W9-BIW-809

Fried

Fried

Surviving Two Centuries
in Restaurants

STEVE LERACH

To Peter.
Best Wishes
Stay Fried
Steve Lerach

BOREALIS
BOOKS

Borealis Books is an imprint of the Minnesota Historical Society Press.

www.borealisbooks.org

© 2008 by the Minnesota Historical Society. All rights reserved. No part of this book may be used or reproduced in any manner whatsoever without written permission except in the case of brief quotations embodied in critical articles and reviews. For information, write to the Minnesota Historical Society Press, 345 Kellogg Blvd. W., St. Paul, MN 55102-1906.

The Minnesota Historical Society Press is a member of the Association of American University Presses.

Manufactured in the United States of America

10 9 8 7 6 5 4 3 2 1

♾ The paper used in this publication meets the minimum requirements of the American National Standard for Information Sciences—Permanence for Printed Library Materials, ANSI Z39.48—1984.

International Standard Book Number
ISBN 13: 978-0-87351-632-7 (cloth)
ISBN 10: 0-87351-632-X (cloth)

Library of Congress Cataloging-in-Publication Data
Lerach, Steve, 1949-
    Fried : surviving two centuries in restaurants / Steve Lerach.
        p. cm.
    ISBN-13: 978-0-87351-632-7 (cloth : alk. paper)
    ISBN-10: 0-87351-632-X (cloth : alk. paper)
    1. Lerach, Steve, 1949- 2. Cooks—United States—Biography. I. Title.

TX649.L47A3 2008
641.5092—dc22
[B]

2008017874

For Ann,
my muse, my editor, my attorney,
and when time permits,
my wife

Publication of this book was supported, in part, with funds provided by Dr. Jason Wong.

Le Menu

Fried

Amuse-bouche

Every night that you're open, you have to make a twenty-four-egg hollandaise. What that means is that every night you need a heavy stainless-steel bowl, a whisk, melted butter, a couple of lemons, cayenne pepper, and two dozen eggs. It's nice if the eggs are room temperature, the scum has been skimmed from the top of the butter, and there is a gently bubbling *bain-marie* for cooking the sauce. Ideal circumstances seldom occur in a restaurant kitchen. You're working a breakneck speed to get ready for the first rush after dealing with late deliveries, physically or mentally absent employees, and inept management that has once again overbooked the dining room for the evening's business. Your hollandaise sauce is just one more piece of the puzzle, and of course, it must be perfect.

You begin cracking your cold eggs into your hand, one at a time. Your fingers are spread just wide enough to allow the white of the egg to drip through while your palm gently cradles the fragile yolk, closing a couple of fingers only enough to pinch off the unfortunate embryo. You toss the globular yolk into the stainless-steel bowl. Repeat twenty-four times. Then shoot a couple ounces of tap water into the bowl and take it over to the stove. Turn a burner onto the lowest setting it can manage, hold the bowl down on the puny flame with one towel-insulated hand, and whip the hell out of the yolk-water mixture with the other. Stir and stir and wait for the mixture to thicken and turn pale, pale yellow. Watch carefully for any lumps forming around the edges, indicating that, even with this pathetic little flame, you're overcooking the sauce and making a bowl of worthless scrambled eggs.

When your yolks form a decent ribbon off the whisk, take them off the fire, throw your towel down on the steel table, and nestle the bowl in the towel. Grab the ladle in the melted butter and simultaneously drizzle a few drops of liquid butter into the eggs while you once again crank with the whisk. If you splash too much butter in now or if the butter is too hot, the mixture will curdle. If you don't stir fast enough, the molten butter will puddle and will not be incorporated into the nascent hollandaise. So you ever-so-slowly introduce the butter, just a few drops at a time, and make sure that every drop is diligently whisked into the whole. Gradually, the added butter triples the volume of the mixture, and you're ready to incorporate the juice of two lemons and your own unique seasoning. If you do everything just right and if the humidity in the kitchen isn't too high and if nobody distracts you during the process and if there's not a trace of any foreign matter on the whisk, the bowl, or your fingers, A MIRACLE OCCURS. The egg yolks and water absorb the butterfat. This mixture in turn absorbs the citric acid and spices and, perhaps, a little sweat from your forehead. *Voilà!* You've created a hollandaise worthy of your asparagus, your bluefish, and the arteries of your customers.

It shouldn't work, but it does. Someone with a modicum of skill combines all sorts of disparate elements. Oil doesn't mix with water; egg yolks should coagulate when touched by direct heat; and the intrusive acid should send all the other elements flying apart. Yet somehow, under intense pressure, all these unique ingredients are tossed together, tossed together and *transformed.*

1

Hors d' Oeuvre

Debut

There is always the smell. I still catch it sometimes while walking by an alleyway on a warm night. The garbage produced by a busy restaurant has a distinctive, unforgettable aroma, and my first experience on my first day on the job was to walk to the back door past a great gaggle of barrels of that garbage, right through that smell. The pungency comes from its many component parts: smoky bacon grease, acrid burnt bread, cigarette butts, coagulating blood, the mellow bite of coffee grounds, and the quick decay of fish parts, all carried directly to the nose on sweet vapors of spilled liquor and stale beer. Naturally, air temperature determines the intensity of the stench, and of course, July 12, 1966, was my first day at the Ambassador.

Unaware of what I was in for, I walked into the kitchen and reported to the harried steward, who had made me fill out a perfunctory application and told me when to show up. He looked at his watch. I was fifteen minutes early. "Go work with Simon until the head dishwasher shows up," he ordered me. "Simon is the potwasher." When the steward saw me looking around in total confusion, he added, "in . . . the . . . potroom," slowly enough so that even a sixteen-year-old kid from the suburbs could understand, and pointed toward an alcove off the main kitchen. From the potroom I could hear clanging, scraping, and not a little cursing.

When I got to the doorway, I saw the back of a small man wearing suspenders and bending over one of the three compartment sinks. His hair was gray and curly, and suds and grease were smeared up his knotted forearms. He was swearing in a soft southern voice, cursing the cooks, the "furrin" chef, and *white* people in general. "Simon?" I interrupted. He turned to face me. Oh my God! Simon was black. And old. Really old. And I had never talked to a black man before.

My sole view of any minority group member had come through the rear window of my family's station wagon as we lit out for the suburbs. Cheap GI mortgages and the fear of people of color had driven a whole generation of young, white World War II vets and their families out of the cities. They headed for the subdivided potato fields and filled-in swamps of suburbia—Eisenhower as Moses leading the Chosen into the desert along a path of interstate concrete.

We found out later we were the boomers, but in those days we were only kids, and there were lots of us. Apparently, killing various European and Asian fascists produced a flood of spermatozoa, which discharged American veterans liberally discharged around the outlands of the subdivisions in the 1950s. Kids were everywhere, and their swarms thickened as you moved closer to the Catholic church in my neighborhood. We all looked alike, wore uniforms to the parochial school, and learned not to question our dads about the war. Everybody just wanted to be normal.

And when one of us reached his teenage years, there was nothing more normal than getting a part-time job. Even if you had been consigned to an expensive all-boys Catholic high school run by the Christian Brothers—holy men who were not wholly men—it was normal to have a job. So when one of my normal white friends recruited me to fill a dishwasher opening at a local suburban motel, I accepted. After all, such temporary employment would provide me with the princely sum of $1.65 per hour, which, after taxes and union dues, would net me enough to contribute some gas money for cruising aimlessly around the suburbs with my friends while listening to the Beach Boys and wishing we knew some girls. Endless summer.

So it was with great shock that I was suddenly presented with a black man of indeterminate antiquity to be my first mentor in a restaurant kitchen. I stared at Simon and then remembered to ask him what I could do to help him. "Well, fust-off, you can tell them dog-ass cooks to stop burnin' evry motherfuckin' thing they touches. Then you can git me a pint o' good whiskey and a big-assed girl and we'll have us a party!" Simon then shook my hand, without wiping his, and asked my name.

"Steve."

"Okay, Gene, let's wash these fuckers and then have us a smoke." So we set to it, scraping and washing and stacking, with Simon giving me directions that barely punctuated the story of his life. His first potwashing job had been in prison in Mississippi where he had bribed a guard to get off the road gang and into the kitchen. What had he been in prison for? Well, just for making the finest moonshine whiskey in the South and also for shooting a G-man who found his still at his shack in the swamp. Seems the cop had seen Simon come to town with an alligator he had killed near the shack, a 'gator that was so big that, when it was slung lengthways on top of an old Ford, both the nose and the tail touched the road. So this revenuer wondered what old Simon was doing that far out in the swamp and came to have a look-see. Shot him in the ass but didn't kill him. Still carried a gun but never killed a man with one. Just with a knife. And by the way, if Gene could find a secret place, Simon and he could set up a still and make some fine whiskey, like he did in the old days when people would come from all over the South to buy a couple of quarts and talk to old Simon!

Of course, now things were different. People didn't know what good whiskey even tasted like. Simon's girlfriend would bring home a bottle of Jim Beam or Old Crow and actually think it was good, but Simon only drank the stuff because he knew that, when she'd had a few drinks, she got mighty friendly, and pretty soon old Simon looked like a young boy riding a bicycle uphill and riding fast (brief demonstration against the pot sink).

When it came time to leave the potroom, I promised Simon I'd be back to help him any time I could. And I meant it. By this time the rest of the crew was arriving at work. There were black people and brown people, men and women of all ages. My direct supervisor, the person who would train me on the intricacies of the big Hobart dish machine, was a surly man in his thirties, the first person with Down's syndrome I had ever met. My partner operating the machine was a kid my own age who had cerebral palsy and could somehow still outwork me and most of the others in the kitchen. My training lasted exactly ten minutes, and then I was submerged in a flood of dirty dishes coming up from the breakfast banquets. The machine hissed and roared, and for three solid hours we toiled away, spraying plates and ashtrays, racking glasses, and passing them into the yawning mouth of the Hobart. The newly washed dishes emerged amid clouds of steam, and each one, at 180 degrees, burned my unprotected hands. My only relief came when I was sent to pick up all the dirty coffee cups from a banquet across the parking lot. The cups were racked and stacked on a dolly, and I couldn't see over the top. So when I hit a hole in the pavement, the whole stack tipped and a couple dozen cups were shattered.

It was then I learned how to sweep with a big push broom. I conducted the cup shards to a big barrel that was already filled with festering, odiferous garbage. Somehow I didn't even notice the smell.

* * *

Your Island in the Sun

In the mid-twentieth century in Minnesota, a land specula-
tor and developer named Oscar Husby had his eye on a four-
and-one-half-acre parcel of vacant land halfway between
downtown Minneapolis and Lake Minnetonka. The Minneapolis suburbs, fueled by cheap gas and cheap GI mortgages,
were rapidly expanding, drawing more and more visitors to
town for business or pleasure. The travelers needed a place to
stay—a clean, safe place, unlike the decaying old hotels downtown or the tawdry cabins of roadside motels. If Husby could
offer an alternative stopping place for the wayfarer, especially
in the upscale, predominantly Jewish St. Louis Park, he knew
the dollars would follow. As part of his vision, Husby insisted, such an establishment would have to be an outgrowth
of his ingrained Norwegian Lutheranism, not to mention his
shrewd business sense. First and foremost, his motor hotel
(not quite a motel, not quite a hotel) would need to cater to
families. No liquor or fleshier temptations would be allowed
on the premises. Rather, a vast hemispheric plastic pleasure
dome would be built over a kidney-shaped swimming pool,
surrounded by guest rooms, real palms, and styrene philo-
dendrons. He would defy the comfortless northern winter
and make vacations in the tropics superfluous with his Island
in the Sun. He would also need to serve food to his customers
and not just the usual Spartan Minnesota fare. Husby insisted
on nice but understandable food prepared by a European chef,
whose presence in the kitchen would guarantee the pedigree of the attached restaurant, the exotic Kashmiri Room.
(Husby had been a supply officer in the China-Burma theater

during the war and liked the word "Kashmiri.") Finally, he would treat all his employees with kindness and generosity, and they in turn would respond with loyalty and hard work. Husby needed a name for his creation, a name that bespoke elegance, old-world charm, and the kind of legitimacy that could rival the hoary downtown hostelries that he intended to outdo. He grandly christened his creation the Ambassador Motor Hotel. It was on Highway 12, but that roadway was always referred to as Wayzata Boulevard (for the benefit of those sensitive of place).

Oscar Husby actually built his vision, his motor hotel, after partnering with another local entrepreneur who could provide a bit of additional seed money to put the project over the top. The new partner already owned a suburban restaurant and entertainment complex modestly known as Diamond Jim's. From his new partner, Husby learned that the idea of opening a hotel-based restaurant without providing alcohol to the patrons was utter lunacy. Husby relented and added the Shalimar Cocktail Lounge into the plans adjacent to the Kashmiri Dining Room. To class things up, when the Ambassador opened in 1963 he had a calligrapher inscribe a scroll, which he hung by the bar entrance. It featured the words to the Edwardian "Kashmiri Song." Had anyone actually read the lyrics, they might have found them a bit incongruous:

> Pale hands I loved beside the Shalimar,
> Where are you now? Who lies beneath your spell?
> Whom do you lead on Rapture's roadway, far,
> Before you agonise them in farewell?

Pale hands, pink tipped, like Lotus buds that float
On those cool waters where we used to dwell,
I would rather have felt them around my throat,
Crushing out life, than waving me farewell!

Rationalizing his purveying of alcoholic beverages, Husby reasoned that the resultant revenues would enhance the value of the Ambassador and therefore allow him to make a more valuable bequest to the Lutheran Church. He could someday rest easily knowing he had permitted only a single, tiny vice.

His new front desk manager soon saw things differently. Frolicking families filled Your Island in the Sun on weekends, but business travelers were a little sparse on that stretch of Highway 12 during the week. The manager's solution to that dilemma consisted of installing several *filles de joie* in inconspicuous guest rooms at the rear of the property and adding an unadvertised hourly rate to the amenities offered. For his role as facilitator, he received a generous gratuity from the ladies in question and simultaneously solved his room vacancy problems. Only years later did it strike Oscar Husby that an occupancy rate of 130 percent was a bit too good to be true.

Though this chicanery was well known to the pampered management and staff of the Ambassador Motor Hotel, no one saw fit to report it to Mr. Husby, so strong was their loyalty—loyalty primarily to whatever scams and deceptions they themselves were running at Mr. Husby's expense. In truth, the wildly popular motor hotel was a Kasbah of lawless behavior. All of Husby's bartenders routinely overcharged their customers, while service employees helped themselves to televisions, janitorial equipment, and various hotel linens. The cooks openly "shopped" in the storeroom, reserving the choicest foodstuffs for themselves and their families or to trade for goods stolen outside their purview. Liquor flowed freely; drugs were dealt in every corner of the property; and more than one amorous staff couple was caught *in flagrante delicto* in guest rooms, storage rooms, or stairwells, while on duty, in or out of uniform. Such were the fringe benefits at Your Island in the Sun.

L'Affaire Boulanger

Selling food is surely the world's second-oldest profession. The hungry customer has provided a livelihood to centuries of restaurateurs, beginning eons before that lofty term was invented. Since everybody has to eat and since the division of labor came to differentiate us from the marsupials, somebody has always been designated to provide the chow and present the bill.

For both the humble and the exalted, staying at home has always meant the consumption of victuals provided by local produce and local talent. But venturing outside the home—be it hovel or palace, the neighborhood, or the political boundaries—has necessitated seeking lunch away from one's hearth. A short trip may have occasioned slinging a skin of wine or a bag of Doritos into the backpack, but journeys of any duration have required other arrangements. Thus, from the earliest times innkeepers and meal purveyors have set up shop alongside trade or invasion routes, eager to exchange carbohydrates for cash (the monotonous food franchises at airport food courts being their spiritual descendants).

The restaurant, as we know it, was a comparatively recent innovation, and of course, the source was French. For over five centuries, "France" and "cuisine" have been largely synonymous. This passion for gustatory excellence has emanated from France since at least the Renaissance, resulting in a highly structured and sophisticated understanding of the vital role that food has played in the country's history and culture. The aristocracy of La Belle France, their fortunes made on enormous tracts of fecund countryside, spent enormous sums on the table's pleasures. Fine food, fine wine, and fine tableside conversation became the identifiers of upper-class French culture. And as in any culture, creation myths abound.

Naturally, we turn to Paris, the epicenter of French life and dining. Lured to the capital and the nearby Palace of Versailles by Louis xiv, much of the French aristocracy spent the early part of the eighteenth century establishing their urban mansions, salons, and kitchen establishments close to the center of absolutism. Their swords seldom called upon to defend a dwindling empire, they instead waged a war of fêtes and entertainments, banquets and balls among themselves. Their household *chefs de cuisine* (executive chefs) marshaled culinary armies of kitchen workers and baggage trains of the finest, rarest wines, liqueurs, and foodstuffs in order to surpass the efforts of rival aristocrats. The great nobles and their great wives—and greater mistresses—paid no taxes, spared no expense, and answered to no one other than the king himself. And the Bourbon kings lived and played and dined more grandly than all the rest, not merely for pleasure but to demonstrate to all that they could.

While crowds flocked to the Tuileries to view the king at dinner, in the streets of Paris things were far different. The common people bought their bread, its price assiduously regulated, from bakers and their cooked meats and stews from licensed *traiteurs,* members in good standing of guilds that had existed since the Middle Ages. Coffee and pastries could be had at the cafés (where a government informant might monitor the caffeinated conversation), or for heartier fare, wine shops abounded. Here the patron would partake of a *table d'hôte* (a limited-choice, fixed-price menu) of dramatically variable quality. In most years foodstuffs were abundant, and the French emulated the aristocrat libertines of the gluttonous First Estate to whatever degree their purses allowed. That's the legend.

The latter half of the eighteenth century brought the height of the Enlightenment. Sense and sensibility were put through a wringer of new ideas. Among the bourgeoisie and the less inbred members of the nobility, odd new thoughts and inclinations took hold, some of them, at least peripherally, involving the dining habits of the enlightened.

The latter half of the eighteenth century also brought the Seven Years' War (1756–1763), which was a disaster for France. Not only did she lose her American colonies, including Canada, but she also incurred crushing war debts, much of the contents of the French treasury being turned over to contractors and victuallers of the business class. Worse, the collision of national misfortune and enlightened sensibilities gave birth to a fashionable craze known as the Cult of Sensitivity. In contrast to the overblown display of the baroque, adherents to this mind-set saw the world through a teary veil of keen perception that doted on the tragic or, more particular, the maudlin side of life. A painting, an opera, or the death of a canary could bring floods of tears, as well as pathetic epigrams weepily memorializing each event. For men who habitually wore mascara, membership in the Cult of Sensitivity was a continual challenge.

These challenges extended to the dinner table. Naturally, the sensitive soul—pale, prone to swooning, and wracked by life's sorrows—needed to show an abstemious countenance and a frail frame. For a member of the aspiring upper-middle classes or of any of the aristocracy's convoluted ranks, this look would have been difficult to accomplish since endless rounds of dinners and parties meant a daily caloric overload—yet another sorrow to be borne. It wouldn't have done to withdraw oneself from these activities, for after all, where was the sense in being a sensitive soul if no one was there to watch? This circumstance has been generally overlooked when the origins of restaurants have been discussed.

Many commentators have, however, repeated the legend that a bourgeois Parisian named Boulanger (various first names were recorded) became a skilled home cook, his specialty a hearty soup made of calf and sheep feet (various animals were recorded). The legend went something like this: Boulanger (or his friends) got the idea that this dish was sufficient to restore the diner's health (or cure his hangover), and the idea of selling this concoction propelled him to open a shop with the word *restaurante* (restorative) on a sign above the door. The people flocked to Boulanger's premises and freely consumed his soup in an atmosphere of *liberté, equalité,* and *fraternité.* But wait—the dark forces of the *ancien régime* (the old, prerevolutionary order), in the guise of the medieval guilds, reacted violently to the revolutionary soup-maker. He was dragged into court for violating the established monopoly of the traiteurs. The ponderous legal machinery chewed on the case for a full five years, but in the end the perplexed judges ruled that the creation of this prototypical restaurant was not, in fact, illegal. Boulanger returned to his shop, rehung his menu, and, pursuant to the Rights of Man, served his greasy potage to all comers. His customers, regardless of title or station, were treated exactly the same within the confines of his establishment, and counts and commoners slurped together. Soon others followed Boulanger's lead, and a restaurant culture was formed. *Vive le pot-au-feu!*

A nice, functional legend. Unfortunately, modern investigators have been unable to find any mention of Boulanger or his restaurant in the annals of French judicial proceedings. It was also not remarked upon by the contemporary press or in the work of diarists of the time. Boulanger can take his place beside Gilgamesh in the dusty files of creation myth.

Logan

Sometime before Husby's Ambassador Motor Hotel was getting up and running, a magistrate in London was handing down a judgment to a delinquent youth of Irish ancestry. The lad in question was barely seventeen but had already been jailed several times for offenses ranging from assault and battery to petty theft and truancy. Life in the East End was rough, and since the boy in question was cursed with a pronounced stammer, he found it easier to employ his fists while negotiating his way. Since a similar judicial body in his home city of Dublin had already prosecuted him for similar offenses, the British judge chose not to extradite him. Instead, he offered the accused an unpalatable choice between spending one year in a juvenile detention facility and enlisting as a cook's apprentice in the merchant marine. John Logan chose to go to sea.

During his first voyage, to India aboard a tramp steamer, Logan's mentor, the ship's cook, fortified himself for a gale with a substantial quantity of cheap brandy. That quantity proved sufficient to make him lose his grip while urgently leaning over the ship's rail, and the old cook was washed overboard. Young Logan sailed into Bombay fully in charge of his first kitchen.

By the time the virtually self-taught Chef Logan returned to England from his maiden voyage, he had learned a great deal about the different cuisines available at the freighter's ports of call. He had acquitted himself well in alcohol-fueled waterfront brawls on at least three continents and acquainted himself with the tender pleasures of the East. Moreover, he was convinced that the life of a chef at sea had a lot going for it. He commanded his own small establishment, was deferred to by the officers and crew, and was able to provide profitable extra rations of food and drink to his shipmates, all at the expense of the ship's owners. At sea he was outside the jurisdiction of the courts, and even his mother at home in Dublin was proud of him.

Back in England, he found that the maritime union was chronically short of trained cooks, and each time he appeared at the hiring hall, he was able to upgrade his employment to nicer ships and more interesting destinations. Aboard ship he worked with cooks from around the world and eagerly absorbed what he could about cuisines and techniques. Shipboard galleys also forced Logan to perfect his sense of timing, organizational skills, and ability to meet numerous daily deadlines. He was receiving his chef's training under fire. Within a few years, he was proficient enough to be hired as a line cook aboard Cunard's flagship, the *Queen Mary,* serving the grandest meals to the grandest clientele, a clientele so grand that they resisted boarding the new jet airliners, which were rapidly making the old luxury liners obsolete.

Many of the kitchen crew aboard the *Queen* were Irish, and Chef Logan fell in with a rough crowd of cronies, with whom he worked and with whom he caroused in seaports on both sides of the Atlantic. It remained a good life. Still, it was unsettling to see fewer and fewer people booking passage on the liners, and rumors of the great ships' demise were daily conversation, along with putative exit strategies for the crew.

On a recent voyage one of Logan's crewmates met a girl from the midwestern United States. Romance flourished, and soon this Irishman was engaged to the girl and planning to leave the *Queen Mary* and resettle in a place called Minneapolis. After a visit to that city with his betrothed, Logan's friend returned with the news that in the middle of nowhere was a prosperous, expanding town trying to make its mark in mid-America. Restaurants were opening there every day, and their proprietors generally felt that the only way to claim they were first-class establishments was to hire a European executive chef.

After docking in New York, Logan collected his pay, jumped ship, and flew to Minneapolis to join his friend, who had landed a job at a local country club. The friend reported that a hotel in St. Louis Park had recently discharged its rage-prone Swiss chef and was looking to replace him with a chef with a better command of the English language. A little stuttering would probably be no obstacle, and since the hotel's upscale dining outlet was called the Kashmiri Room, the ownership felt it was important for the incoming chef to have some passing knowledge of Indian cuisine. After all, the restaurant had always maintained one (and only one) curry dish on its menu.

John Logan always carried himself well. A big man in several different dimensions, he had thriftily had suits tailored for him when his ship was docked in Hong Kong. He had shirts made for pennies in India and bought fashionable bow ties in London. He even owned a bowler hat but wore it only under duress, to job interviews for example. Thus attired, he

appeared in Oscar Husby's office to interview for the executive chef position. Logan must have seemed a godsend to the
old Norwegian. Husby was wearing the white patent-leather
shoes and belt that he sported from Memorial Day to Labor
Day. Sartorially, he resembled all other members of the local Rotary Club, who held their weekly luncheon meeting at
the Ambassador. Now, Husby was confronted by an imposing, splendidly dressed, and plainly cultured gentleman who
just happened to be seeking to direct the feeding of him and
his fellow Rotarians. For his part Logan had remembered to
medicate his chronic stammer with a tumbler of vodka just
before the interview. They got along famously. John Logan
was hired to be the third (European) executive chef of the
Ambassador Motor Hotel.

He was my first boss, my first executive chef. I was a
dishwasher, and naturally, he despised me.

The Restaurant Is Born

According to historian Rebecca Spang, in *The Invention of
the Restaurant,* the actual inventor of the restaurant was a
Frenchman named Mathurin Roze de Chantoiseau. Roze de
Chantoiseau was a polymath who was later to bring a plan for
eliminating France's national debt to the king's ministers.
(The plan might have worked, but since it was submitted in
1789, events pretty much overtook the idea.) Roze de Chantoiseau also ran an information office and edited a gazette, much
of which was dedicated to differing views on exactly what was

wrong in France. Chief among the many contentions was the parlous state of the cooking available to the masses, particularly in Paris. Certainly, great chefs existed, but they served almost entirely in the manses of the aristocracy, and only in those sumptuous surroundings could true cuisine be found.

For the French, interest in food was not the peculiar preoccupation of a few enthusiasts but rather a component of the broad range of interests that made up a part of being involved in cultural, social, and political life. In the 1760s, most prominent French thinkers were fascinated by cooking and drew moral and medical conclusions from the state of gastronomy in the country. Taste was seen as a universal virtue, and the tastes for art, science, and food were regarded as inextricably intermingled. Cuisine joined mesmerism, clandestine publications, adultery, and the state of the French polity as subjects of fascination and conversation. And as with these other popular enthusiasms, there was much quackery to be found in the culinary realm.

The purported medicinal properties of certain foods were the subject of intellectual speculation. Specifically, it was thought that concentrated and prolonged cooking of various ingredients, primarily proteins, would yield healthful wonder foods that would restore physical well-being and optimize body function. Theorists, most prominently Roze de Chantoiseau, postulated that large-scale adoption of this dietary regime would increase agricultural production and improve commerce. The only obstacle to supplying these salubrious concoctions was that no one seemed ready to start such a new and unorthodox venture.

Roze de Chantoiseau did an end run around the strictures that defined the positions of traiteurs and tavern keepers in Parisian commercial life. Using his influence with the king's ministers, in January 1768 he purchased an official commission as one of twelve cook-caterers who followed the court. This commission exempted Roze from most of the licensing restrictions and requirements that dogged his erstwhile competitors and gave tacit royal sanction to his endeavors. He then opened a shop to serve the healthful bouillons on rue Sainte-Honoré. Since Roze, in another of his many endeavors, was also preparing to publish his *Almanach general,* listing all seven hundred places where food was available to a hungry customer in Paris, he placed several prominent listings therein for "Le Restaurateur Roze," "Rue Saint Honoré," and "Hôtel d'Aligre." Here, the anonymously authored *Almanach* raved, could be found all the choicest, most delicate, and healthful soups, prepared to the most exacting standards. Here could a customer be seated and offered a choice of delights. Here could persons of all backgrounds dine together in an atmosphere enjoying both the blessing of the king and the benefits of the latest scientific knowledge as guarantors of quality.

For adherents to the Cult of Sensitivity, such an establishment seemed a godsend. Instead of nibbling *petit fours* in the salons of the decadent aristocracy or ingesting whatever nondescript *ragout* the local cookshop was peddling, the hungry but abstemious cultist could have an entirely unique experience. Though he might water his broth with earnest weeping, the Sensitive One would be able to display his isolation in public, pondering the world's cruel usages while not adding any superfluous poundage to his quaking frame. He could sate his debased physical hunger while restoring the energy needed to navigate this vale of tears. He could show his differentiation from the common herd at a mere cost of three to six *livres* per bowl. Roze de Chantoiseau's restaurant was an instant success and spawned dozens of imitators in the first few years of operation.

Not-so-Quick Bread

Dylan Thomas termed them "Professional Irishmen" when he visited America, and Chef John Logan without a doubt epitomized the breed. He could switch into a stutterless, leprechaunish brogue when the situation demanded and pine for the old sod with the best of them. His favorite credential for proving his Irishness was his mass producing of Irish soda bread whenever the occasion demanded. This feat was relatively easy as he had a staff of ad hoc Hibernians working in the Ambassador's kitchen, dreading another Irish soda bread challenge. Thus, mounds of the crumbly stuff could be produced for every Irish festival, wedding, or wake without so much as a dusting of flour touching the chef's starched jacket.

Creating this delicacy required merely a thirty-quart Hobart mixer, a line of ovens, a dozen aluminum sheet pans, and forearms made of titanium. All the wet ingredients were thrown into the mixing bowl, followed by all the dry. Then the mixer, its bowl filled to the brim, was cautiously turned on. The first revolution of the paddle always deposited about a pint of the mixture onto the unhappy cook's shoes, which prompted him to quickly turn off the machine and reach for a rubber spatula in order to rearrange the ingredients. At this point he naturally wondered whether the portion that had made it onto the floor contained anything vital for making the recipe work. No one, to my knowledge, was able to resist the temptation of brushing his shoes off above the mixing bowl just to make things right.

Once the mixer, in fits and starts, had completed its job, the dough was turned out onto a heavily floured tabletop. At this stage the stuff was viscous and ambulatory and prone to running toward the table edge if not forcefully corralled and contained. Here the mass of dough—now about the size and shape of one of those gigantic tortoises my friends and I used to torture at the zoo—would rest for a minute or two or for at least the time it took to run outside and smoke a furtive cigarette. Nerves calmed, the cook returned to do battle with the incipient soda bread.

The next phase involved the cook's plunging his hands into the seething mass and scooping out one-and-a-half- to one-and-three-quarter-pound clods of the stuff, as measured by a flimsy portion scale, and his somehow turning each of them into a loaf of bread. This was where Herculean forearms came in handy, if the cook had them (I didn't), because the recalcitrant dough had to be folded and kneaded and slapped and squeezed until it resembled a much smaller tortoise, its head and limbs prudently withdrawn to avoid the chaos. Chef Logan, who had hands the size of bunches of bananas, could effortlessly form two loaves simultaneously. The rest of us mortals struggled with one at a time.

When the last of the dough was panned up on rows of baking sheets and the clinging remains were scraped from the fingers, what was allegedly the most important part of the preparation took place. A slit was made in the dough before baking, which allowed the internal moisture an escape route, and those slits had to be done in the form of a cross. Logan had instructed us, as he had been instructed, to "say a f-f-fucking prayer" with every cut, or the bread would refuse to rise. Since we always suspected that at least part of the baking soda was in the portion of the mix that hit the floor, the prayer seemed like a reasonable precaution. A ruined batch of soda bread often had dire consequences in Chef Logan's kitchen.

Once the first batch was safely in the oven, the ingredients for subsequent batches could be assembled. If there was a major Irish event in town, four or five batches per shift were the norm. Soda bread days did chafe Chef Logan in that he needed to attend the entire operation. The rule was that only the chef could pronounce whether the loaves of bread were actually done, a judgment made through a series of visual inspections and, more important, the thump test. Logan, usually barehanded, would remove a loaf from the oven and hold it to his ear while delivering a series of gentle thumps to its crusty bottom. If and only if the proper holy hollow sound was heard, the soda bread was removed from the oven and cooled. Then the next batch was baked until its thumping time. In fact, after each batch emerged, we cooks all thumped a loaf or two, trying to discover the arcane code that signaled the successful creation of a loaf of Irish soda bread.

2

Entrée

Among the Cooks

It doesn't take long for a person to get sick and tired of washing dishes, especially in a busy restaurant. Although the multifarious personalities of the crew, the complicated nature of the operation, and even the workings of the immense Hobart dish machine all had their charms, the work itself well and truly sucked, which, combined with the *suckiest* imaginable experience—incarceration in high school—made for a rather bleak existence. Clearly, I needed to escape from something, and graduation seemed like it was years away. And there, behind a high, stainless-steel counter, was the world of the cooks.

At any given moment, at least a dozen of them were working away in the kitchen. At first they all seemed interchangeable, a raucous, profane cast whose sole interaction with the dish crew was to scream for stacks of scalding-hot dishware—dinner plates, B&BS, soup bowls, monkey dishes, salad plates, goosenecks, casseroles, platters, ramekins, and parfaits. As I delivered the goods into their infernal realm, I began to differentiate their jobs, their names, and their functions.

There were many major divides. The first was the nature of their preparations: hot and cold. Generally, the men cooked the hot food, and the women attended to the cold preparations. Then there were the line cooks, who prepared the à la carte meals for the Kashmiri Dining Room, as opposed to the banquet crew, who produced vast quantities of identical foods for large parties, along with dreadfully large quantities of dirty dishes and utensils. Finally, a different uniform designated the coffee shop cooks, who slammed out short-order dishes in their own little kitchen down the hall from the main arena. All this was presided over by an executive chef and a couple of assistants, known as sous-chefs. (When I first heard this title, I assumed that these individuals were Oglalas or Minneconjous, until I discovered by some accident that the proper spelling of their title was not "Sioux.")

This group was an intimidating one to any outsider. First of all, these people actually *knew* how to do things and always seemed to be furiously busy doing them. Second, they seemed to have their own language, giving names to people, actions, and objects that the uninitiated could only understand after observation and familiarity. It would not do to ask for clarification, and anyone confessing ignorance of their arcane lexicon was raucously and profanely ridiculed. This risk of humiliation led to some awkward moments and a few near misses. A novice might be dispatched to fetch a nonexistent left-handed ladle or a "meat stretcher." I recall vainly searching the dictionary for the meaning of "bamperine" only to find out months later that the nonword was a corruption of the French *bain-marie,* basically a steam table. I also discovered that every cook took offense at being called a shoemaker, which was a French-originated term of derision for Italians in general and bad cooks in particular. Worse was being termed a Greek, which meant, well, a Greek, or a cook prone to producing overly oily, sloppy food. To be derided as a Greek shoemaker, usually with a few selected profanities, was simply anathema.

Generally, though, the male cooks spoke in an argot composed primarily of profanities and obscenities. Pans and spoons were "male" or "female," depending on whether they had holes or not, and sauces were "douches," as in, "Put some douche over that turkey and send it the hell out, you fuckin' shoemaker!" Garbage receptacles were "shit cans," small flexible knives were "boners," and woe unto the dumb ass who didn't understand what they were talking about.

As a dumb ass, I was expected to do whatever the people in the white jackets wanted, which centered on the endless washing, carrying, sweeping, and mopping that kept the kitchen running. On occasion, when a large party was to be served, I was pulled off the dish crew to help on the assembly line that plated hundreds of lunches and dinners at breakneck speed. A long stainless-steel table was set up with stacks of hot dinner plates at one end and an empty, closed cart at the other. In between stood as many cooks as necessary, each with his contribution to the finished meal: potatoes, vegetables, sauces, garnishes. As a plate was shoved by, each contributed his offering, and the finished dinner had a stainless-steel cover clanged onto it just as it was shoved into the cart. When drafted onto these crews, I was certainly never allowed to touch actual food, as a rigid hierarchy regulated who did what in these situations. The chef in charge always handled the meat portion, to be placed in the center of the plate. Cooks of lesser status then added the accompaniments, checked the plate for completeness, wiped up any spills, and then—and only then—was a dumb ass allowed to burn himself on the hot plate as he covered it and put it into the wagon. Still, the whole experience gave me a chance to work with the cooks, especially since the other dishwashers I worked with were either congenitally slow-witted or had cerebral palsy and thus were liabilities on the fast-paced dishing line. As hectic as such an operation could be, I cherished these brief respites from the dish room's drudgeries.

The first of the cooking crew who had spoken to me was Miss Del, the head pantry cook. In absolute charge of all cold food, she was a veteran, stooped-over black woman whose competence, not to mention raw orneriness, elicited the respect of all the workers in the Ambassador's kitchen. On my first day she had taken me aside, asked my name, and given me her Two Commandments:

I. Speak when you're spoken to;
II. Clean up your own mess.

As long as I followed Del's commandments, we got along fine. Soon we were talking regularly, and one day I confessed that I'd like to do something in the kitchen which didn't involve washing dishes. Was there ever going to be an opening in the cold-food pantry?

"Stevie, honey, you can't work over here, though we'd love to have you. Pantry work is for women. You need to work with the hot-food cooks. Now, I know you're afraid of that stuttering chef [I blushed], but you don't need to ask him for anything. Have you noticed that every day the storeroom guy throws a fifty-pound sack of onions out on the prep table? The cooks are supposed to peel those whenever they get a chance, and they HATE IT! Well, if you was to just go over and ask them if you could help with the peeling, they might just give you some other jobs too, and pretty soon you're off the dishwasher!" This seemed liked reasonable advice.

When I first asked Bob, one of the cooks, whether he needed a hand with the onions, it was an inadvertent masterpiece of timing. Bob was plainly hungover that morning, reeking of stale booze and old tobacco and truculent in a fatalistic sort of way. (These symptoms were not unusual among the cooks.) All morning the other cooks had been sneaking up behind him and noisily dropping pots and pans, farting, or making foul remarks that set his stomach churning. The onions weren't helping either, so Bob was more than happy to turn part of the job over to me. When I asked him if

I could borrow a knife, he motioned me over to his toolbox and told me to use his boner. I opened the lid of the box, the inside of which bore the scrawl THE ONLY THING LOWER THAN A COCKSUCKER IS A THEEF. Reaching in for the knife, I disturbed a towel and discovered that it was wrapped around Bob's .38, snuggled in with the cook's beat-up tools. It seems that a jealous husband had been threatening Bob, and he thought it only prudent to have a piece within easy reach. Since several of the other cooks regularly packed heat, Bob's weapon was in no way an aberration, other than in the way it cohabited with the spatulas and cutlery.

With Bob's boner I set to work on the onions. The juice of the big Bermudas zeroed in on my hay fever, and I was weeping by the time I finished the second onion. But since I was back with the cooks and *actually touching food,* a few of them came and talked to me. I even got to participate in one of their time-honored rituals. Two of the hot-food cooks, Tony and Bill, weighed well over three hundred pounds apiece, most of it around the midsection. At least once a day one or the other of them would come around a corner or proceed down the same narrow aisle and confront the other. Squaring off, the two would proceed to bump bellies and then repeat the process again and again, harder and harder, until one gave way. This was as savage and unrelenting as elks in a rutting frenzy.

This day the two of them winked at each other and then sandwiched me in the middle of their belly battle for about a dozen bumps. I laughed, I shouted, all the while crying from the onions. Hearing the uproar, the executive chef stalked out of his office, looked at me, and said, "What the f-f-fuck is *he* doing back here?"

Elsewhere, others were trying to find their proper place. One of them begins his own story here.

Michael Tells His Story

Well, it's about time. People certainly ignore you when you're on the wrong side of the sod. God knows I wouldn't have let that happen before. Of course, sometimes I had to remind them that I was more of a man than they'd ever be, and more of a woman than any of them would ever have.

Oh, my story.

Born in 1948. My father was a colonel in the marines or air force or some bullshit, so we moved around a lot. When I was about twelve, we settled down to live in Chippewa Falls, Wisconsin, which I would call the Asshole of the World if I didn't think saying that was an insult to all assholes everywhere.

My family was *very* Catholic, so they made me go to the parish school and be an altar boy. About the third time I served Mass, the priest hit on me, and I was too scared to say no (saying no has always been a problem for me). Well, Father Joe pretty much fucked me from then on all the way through high school, and when I told him I didn't know what to do after graduation, he said I should settle down and get married. After all, you couldn't be gay in Chippewa Falls.

I had met this girl at church; her father was a big shot at

the bank, and she was nice but really spoiled, and she liked me well enough. So we had a big wedding in 1967, with Father Joe doing the honors after doing *me* the night before. My father-in-law helped us get a decent little house, just like all the other breeders—and then I got my draft notice.

But I was really happy about that. I thought, OK you're married now, and all you have to do is go to war and then you'll BE A REAL MAN, and you can stop looking at every cute stud in town and not even be tempted to sneak over to the rectory for a blow job. Everybody in town was happy for me because, just before I went off to boot camp, I found out that my wife was pregnant, so at least if I was killed, they wouldn't have to change the population sign at the edge of town.

I found out that the way to straightness didn't involve going over to Vietnam and hanging out with thousands of other lonely, muscular guys. I did my duty. Of course, I got hassled now and then by queer-hating rednecks. One day our squad was unloading a big stack of lumber off a two-and-a-half-ton truck when one of the rednecks in the company threw a long two-by-four my way when I wasn't looking, and the fucking thing caught me right in the mouth. It knocked all my front teeth out and put me in the hospital for a long time. That's how I won my Purple Heart (I think I traded the medal for a cocktail sometime later).

While I was in the hospital waiting for my mouth to heal, and for U.S. Army dentures, I really did a lot of thinking. Here I was in this stinking jungle, living a lie. Living a double lie actually. I was not a soldier; I wasn't even a husband. I was running away from being a fag, a fag with a kid on the way.

I guess I got pretty depressed, but I decided that, when my tour was up, I was going back to Chippewa Falls (even *that* shithole looked good now) and just be square with everybody. I worked out an administrative discharge with the army by blackmailing my CO (I think you know how) and headed back to the World.

So when I got home, I had this cute little baby girl waiting for me, and everybody was happy that everything but my mouth was in one piece. They threw a welcome-home party for me, and as usual I had too much to drink, and I told them. My parents, my wife, her parents. I told them all that I was gay and that was that. No more pretending, no more lying. Then they weren't so happy.

My wife took the baby that night and moved in with her parents, and the bank took back the house. My "dad" took a swing at me (he missed; he was drunk, too) and told me that if I knew what was good for me, I'd better leave town and never come back. The next day I did just that. And I haven't been back.

Like every other small-town faggot in the Midwest, I headed for Minneapolis.

Revolution

Aside from the growth of the restaurant industry, the last three decades of the eighteenth century were unkind to France. Citizens of all classes could rendezvous in eateries and discuss the calamities of lost wars, the government's

financial malfeasance, and the strangling effects of the ancien régime's social order. After all, the Second Estate (the
clergy) paid only 2 percent of their massive income in taxes.
The First Estate (the hereditary aristocracy) paid nothing. The Third Estate (basically everybody else) shelled out
a whopping 50 percent of their incomes to the tax collector.
The educated middle class *(bourgeoisie)* became increasingly
restive in spite of their detached Cult of Sensitivity—more
fodder for conversation over one's pot-au-feu.

Another lively topic was the new republic across the
Atlantic. That innovation had been guaranteed by French
blood and treasure during the American Revolution, a war
that found France on the winning side while suffering the
loss of further fleets, armies, and colonies in the final settle-
ment. Furthermore, talk of the irony of Frenchmen fighting
to liberate foreigners from the rule of a foreign monarch,
while their own king retained his despotic powers at home,
allowed many a meal to grow cold. Vilified as one of the most
ineffectual monarchs ever to stumble across the European
stage, Louis xvi and the entire Bourbon dynasty would be
swept away in the fury of the French Revolution, beginning
in July 1789. This upheaval made its American predecessor
look like a rather bland appetizer.

The documentation of the wrenching transformation of
French society and government in those years has provided
plentiful sustenance to novelists and historians for generations. Few of these have acknowledged the role of restaurants proper as gathering places for the successive waves of
factions that embroiled Paris and the rest of the country in

revolutionary activities. As reform-minded delegates to the Estates-General flooded into the capital, they fueled their deliberations over food and wine in these establishments. An early revolutionary martyr, Le Pelletier, was assassinated by a royalist as he dined in Fevrier's restaurant. The table where he took his last meal became a shrine, and his moderate repast was made an icon of proper republicanism.

Overindulgence was now associated with the discredited ruling class. Shipments of foodstuffs into Paris dropped off as frugality and uncertainty combined to discourage purveyors. When the supply of bread ran out in the city, mobs of its inhabitants marched to Versailles and seized the king and his family, bringing them back to Paris accompanied by the royal guard, who had joined the insurgents. Louis and his family were placed under house arrest as more and more aristocrats tested the wind and headed for the border. Obviously, things were getting out of hand.

The incident that turned the revolutionary tide inexorably against the king occurred on June 21, 1791, when, as restaurant-savvy Parisians put it, Louis attempted to run out on the check. At the urging of the queen, Louis disguised his family and, with a few loyalists, boarded a coach and made a run for the frontier. He was hoping to reach the territory of his decidedly monarchy-friendly brother-in-law, the emperor of Austria. He nearly made a clean escape, but Louis was a renowned gourmand, and hunger overtook him before the authorities in Paris could. He ordered his carriage to stop in the town of Varennes in Champagne in order to refresh himself in the establishment of a man named Sauce. While the monarch was dining on a platter of pigs' feet, he was recognized by the local postmaster, who was familiar with the royal portrait from the stamps he sold. The alarm was given, and Louis and his party were duly arrested. He was allowed to finish his supper before being dragged back to Paris.

Revolutionary propagandists made much of the king's flight to Varennes. Clearly, he had been abandoning France in its hour of need, going over to the enemy, as autocratic governments throughout Europe ranged themselves against the revolutionary upstarts in Paris. Caricatures of the king at his last meal outside of captivity showed him as a porcine libertine, the husband of the reputedly immoral Austrian whore Marie Antoinette. Before Varennes, France had been struggling toward a constitutional monarchy. Louis xvi's arrest on Sauce's premises condemned that idea and, ultimately, the king himself. These stories mutated and spread throughout the nation and were increasingly associated with the unique French institution, the restaurant.

Michael Continues His Story

Even I was shocked by what I found in Minneapolis. It seems like everybody came out of the closet at once in the late sixties and early seventies. Being gay was finally cool, and a lot of us just went wild. There were a bunch of new bathhouses operating in town, and at least five nights a week, I'd start the evening with cocktails at the Gay 90's and then head over to Big Daddy's Bathhouse. Most of us felt like we had just been liberated, or let out of fag jail or something.

Without much in the way of skills, I had to find work that would get me enough money to live and also not get in the way of my nightly activities. Restaurants were a natural for me and for lots of others. Just about every nice place had gay waiters, and all you needed to get a job were good manners and a willingness to hustle, and believe me, I knew how to hustle. Manners were the problem. I lost a couple of jobs because I told the asshole customers exactly what I thought of them.

But in the end, in restaurants nobody much cares about where you're from or who you're sleeping with. The only thing that mattered is whether you could do the job or not. Even if I was a bitchy waiter, there were always other jobs that needed doing. I got some experience doing short-order cooking and cold food in a couple of places and did some bartending too. I worked nights because getting up in the morning has always been a problem for me, especially if I wake up next to some sissy whose name I can't even remember. The only thing I was ever sure of was that I had met him the night before in a bar or a restaurant.

Dining in the Shadow of the Guillotine

On the morning of October 16, 1793, the executioner reached into the basket below the blade of the guillotine and retrieved the head of Marie Antoinette, recently retired queen of France. As he held the grisly trophy aloft for the jeering spectators, the headsman jammed a piece of cake into the lifeless royal mouth. The crowd roared its approval. Many of them recalled the words the queen had spoken before the

Revolution. When Marie was told that the people of Paris had no bread and quipped, "Let them eat cake," she had actually recommended the far less cakey *brioche* for the starving masses, but the howling mob, in this instance anyway, was disinclined to quibble about the menu.

Besides, there were plenty of places where the menu could be a source of debate and concern. Though money was short and victuals scarce in revolutionary Paris, restaurants continued to flourish in the French capital. Members of the constituent assembly flocked to Beauvilliers, where the wine selection was reputedly the finest in Paris. Meot offered more than one hundred dishes on its menu, and the republic's constitution of 1793 was drawn up in that establishment's private rooms. Perhaps the finest meals of all could be had at Les Trois Frères Provençaux, which had, before the upheavals of 1789, existed as a modest hole-in-the-wall serving decidedly mediocre fare. With the overthrow of the Old Regime, Les Provençaux moved to the fashionable Gallerie de Beaujolais, overlooking the gardens of the Palais-Royal, and packed in the customers seeking its savory Mediterranean dishes. Restaurants had never been more popular.

This was in itself a bit surprising. With tumbrels full of condemned aristocrats rolling through the streets of Paris, foreign armies massing on the borders, and large sections of the country in open revolt against a regicidal central government, it seemed unlikely that any business segment, other than the mortuaries, could prosper. Yet Paris restaurants reached new heights of expertise and acclaim. There was even a lively catering business serving imprisoned nobles

waiting for their trips to the guillotine. All sorts of delicacies were delivered to the condemned, oftentimes prepared
by the same hands that had served these aristocrats before
their condemnation. The pleasures of the table were all that
remained for the displaced—and doomed—First Estate.

Those who had, in happier times, provided such pleasures for the nobility now did so under their own auspices.
The *chefs de cuisine, rôtisseurs* (roast cooks), *sauciers* (sauté
cooks), and *pâtissiers* (pastry cooks) who had manned the
culinary establishments of the aristocracy suddenly found
themselves out of work as the Revolution roiled toward its
inevitable, bloody conclusion. Their employers had either
fled the country or been frog-marched to prison, leaving
kitchen staffs bereft of employment. They had little choice
but to find a place in the burgeoning restaurant industry.

In actuality a few pioneering chefs had made this transition in the decade before the Revolution. Antoine Beauvilliers was a notable example. He left the service of a branch
of the Bourbon family when they were forced to downsize
their staff, owing to the family's financial mismanagement.
His establishment, set up in a property hastily sold off by a
fugitive aristocrat, soon became a popular dining spot. Its
popularity continued through the Revolution and into the
nineteenth century.

Once the Revolution had begun, a flood of new talent
reached Paris's kitchens. For some the transition was far from
smooth. Gabriel Charles Doyen, Marie Antoinette's personal
chef, went to the guillotine in 1794, charged with longing for
the Old Regime and missing his former employers. Some

chefs were seen as *too* connected to their aristocratic employers and were brought along by those nobles who had the good fortune to flee the country. Thus they traveled with their patrons to any city in Europe that would welcome such exiles, and some made it as far as the émigré outpost of New Orleans, where they added their talents to a new nation's cuisine.

In some sense, this shift of employment mirrored the movement away from the patronage of European creative artists popular throughout the latter part of the eighteenth century. Visual artists, writers, composers, and now chefs struck out from their dependence on the whims of noble patrons and into the competitive arena of public performance. Though the upheaval of the Revolution accelerated the process for chefs, the institution of the restaurant had already begun that transition. Moreover, this new merit-based competition among restaurateurs continued and enhanced the democratic nature of the restaurant.

Miss Del Lays into Logan

I didn't witness the confrontation, but a couple people later told me that it had been pretty heated. After I was sent packing to the dish area, Miss Del charged into Chef Logan's office and told him in no uncertain terms that she was not going to go on working overtime forever just because he couldn't find her any help to set up the Sunday brunch every week, and furthermore, there was this kid who had been peeling onions who really wanted to learn how to do food, and she would be more than happy to train him, and it was a goddam shame that somebody could come over to this country and have some opportunity and then turn around and deny it to somebody else just because he didn't like him, and since nobody could figure out *why* he didn't like him, he oughta wonder if he wasn't just some dumb foreigner who didn't know shit from Shinola, but one thing he oughta know was that Del *and all her recipes* were leaving the Ambassador unless she got some help, and she meant soon.

The chef stuttered out o-o-o-k and told the steward to replace me on the dish machine. Del winked at me as she returned to her station.

Stuffed: The Inca's Revenge

For Atahualpa, the last ruler of the Inca Empire, August 29, 1533, proved to be a pretty bad day. Despite providing Francisco Pizarro and his conquistadors with a ransom of a roomful of gold and two others filled with silver, the Great Inca was strangled to death by the Spaniards, as a prelude to their conquest of Peru. Things could have been worse. Atahualpa had recently renounced his native gods and converted to Christianity. According to the church, he could then lawfully succumb to the garrote rather than be burned at the stake as a heretic. Once again, the rule of law served to protect us from our darker impulses.

Shockingly, the Europeans did not offer the Incas a refund on the ransom already paid. Instead, the proceeds went toward purchasing altarpieces, whips, and leg irons for use in civilizing the latest province of New Spain. However quickly the treasure was spent, the true wealth that came from beneath the Peruvian soil was vegetable rather than mineral. The discovery of the potato changed European cuisine almost overnight.

Here was a crop that was hardy, nutritious, and versatile. It could be eaten by all classes, made into a passable spirit, or used as cheap fodder for livestock. In short order the potato flourished from County Cork to the Urals and then recrossed the Atlantic during the second century of European incursion onto the North American continent.

And there the potato died a horrible death in the kitchens of mid-twentieth-century America. The humble potato was an integral part of every meal, whether baked, fried, boiled, shredded, diced, drowned in polypropylene cheese sauce, or steamed to translucence. But of all the ways concocted to use or abuse the potato, none could be more dastardly, debilitating, or depraved than the baked stuffed potato, aka the twice-baked potato. And each of us who saw this item listed on a banquet production sheet had his own personal, obscene term for it.

At the Ambassador we had a catering manager who delighted in padding the guest check by selling his customers the enhancement of baked stuffed (BS) potatoes on party menus. For just an additional dollar, the guest could be served an elegant BS potato alongside the main course, instead of the usual inert, foil-wrapped spud. Think of the delight that four hundred revelers at a wedding banquet might find in devouring the very best BS potatoes on Highway 12! No fussing with foil wrappers or bowls of sour cream. No burden of having to wield salt and pepper shakers to make the baker palatable. No burnt lips or tongues from potatoes that actually held their heat. A real BS potato for only a measly dollar more. The things practically sold themselves.

For the cook who drew the assignment of producing the BS potatoes, life held few delights. First, he had to go searching for enough conventional baked potatoes to complete his work. At the Ambassador we routinely collected all the leftover baked potatoes at the end of each dinner shift. The overproduced potatoes were stashed in the walk-in cooler to await reincarnation. If the cook could find enough of them—half as many as the guest count—he was in business. If not, he would have to actually bake some raw potatoes in order to produce the BS, an unfortunate additional task and expense.

Each potato was then split lengthwise with a knife, and the grayish-tan innards were scooped out and discarded. Once baked and chilled, the flesh of mealy russet baking potatoes gets crumbly and smelly, and only the stuffable skins are of any value. These were laid out in yawning rows on a pan to await further insult.

This insult came in the form of the stuffing used to fill the BS potatoes. The cook estimated how much milk to heat on the stovetop, and if the milk did not scald while he hurriedly smoked a cigarette, it was transferred to a thirty-quart-capacity bowl mounted on a Hobart mixer. The cook then opened several no. 10 cans of dehydrated whipped-potato mix and began feeding their contents into the milk while the mixing paddle slowly whirled about. If the task was not done carefully, equal amounts of potato mix reached both the milk and the floor. Usually, after considerable scraping and cursing by the cook, this bland cocktail reached a state approximating mashed potatoes. But the magic had only begun.

Five-pound tubs of sour cream made their appearance, and their contents were incorporated into the mixture. A pile of bacon, left over from breakfast, came next after being finely chopped. (Occasionally, an unwary cook tried to cut corners by sneaking in Bacos from the salad department. The food coloring in the artificial soy-bacon substitute inevitably turned the resulting glop a lurid pink.) The cook also opened a can of freeze-dried chives for inclusion. On opening, the chives smelled like an old tomb, powdery and rancid, but in they went. Next, raw egg yolks were added to bind and enrich the mixture, as was just enough salt and white pepper. A final adjustment for consistency may have required some more whipped-potato mix, and a two-finger taste completed the process—the mixing process, that is.

The task of shuttling this mélange into the listless skins remained. The preferred tool was a large pastry bag, a conical canvas tube with a toothed metal tip at the pointy end, which served as the orifice from which stuffing flowed. The amalgam was then scooped into the big end of the tube and squeezed out the small end. A few wrist and finger gyrations imparted attractive swirls and curls to each BS potato, but just as often some particle refused to smoothly pass through the tip and the cook had to exert more pressure on the bag to move the recalcitrant lump. The resultant tube fart blasted a little extra mix into the shell and onto its neighbors and the cook's apron. Strangling a pastry tube for hours was exhausting and often made for a bad day.

The finished BS potatoes were drizzled with melted butter and dusted with parmesan cheese. Thus adorned, they returned to the cooler to await immolation in the oven and service to the unsuspecting. Each simple, nutritious potato had been augmented with bacon and butterfat, and milk, cream, cheese, egg yolks, and dehydrated carbohydrates laid in ambush for the descendants of the European colonizers. Somewhere, perhaps outside a cardiac ward, Atahualpa the Great Inca is smiling.

3

Poisson

Chef Logan's Kingdom

Chef John Logan soon discovered what a good situation he had as chef of the Ambassador Motor Hotel. The property generated a hefty profit, and as long as that was the case, Mr. Husby did not apply much scrutiny to the operation. To compound the undersight, the general manager had been promoted from the accounting office, and he understood little beyond the ledger books. This left Chef Logan free to run things as he saw fit without fear of functional control from the front office. Chefs in their own kitchens tend to be independent and autocratic, and the situation at the Ambassador allowed Logan even more leeway than most. The only slight restraint on his authority was the union contract that covered

his workers. The hotel and restaurant workers' union, enfee-
bled by utter corruption, was easily circumvented, however.
Besides, the business agent who visited the Ambassador was
another Irish immigrant and a crony and regular cotippler of
the chefs.

The Irish connection opened a great many doors. In cahoots with a crew of other Hibernian expatriates, Logan
formed a group called the Sons and Daughters of Ireland.
This "charitable" organization promoted Irish culture and
food and the Irish Republican Army, the last in ostensible
secrecy. In an era before homegrown, legalized charitable
gambling, it sold worthless tickets for the Irish Sweepstakes,
pocketing a good share of the proceeds but always skimming
off the top for the cause. Twice a year Chef Logan would fly to
Ireland to visit his sainted mother, and on those occasions
he would go through customs with as much as $250,000 for
the IRA taped to his massive body.

Oscar Husby was a savvy promoter, so it was with some
satisfaction that he arranged for his chef to have a continuing presence on a local TV show. Each week Chef Logan
brought a load of ingredients to the station and, overcoming
his stammer with vodka, produced some delicacy on camera
while the hostess of the program cooed her delight. Logan
also provided recipe cards for the viewers, which led many of
them to contact him for catered events. Those who wished to
use the facilities at the Ambassador became new customers
for Mr. Husby. Those who wished to have a celebrity appearance by Chef Logan in their very own homes got their wish as
well, for a substantial fee, without Husby's knowledge of that

fee or the cost of the ingredients quietly removed from the Ambassador's food inventory.

Other kitchen employees, inspired by their chef's success, emulated him in any number of similar scams and pilferages. At times the Ambassador's illicit external catering must have equaled the amounts that actually showed up on the books. At the very least the Ambassador's kitchen staff and their families and consorts dined sumptuously at a very reasonable cost.

The staff was fairly typical of the time and place. Most were industry veterans who fancied themselves as free agents, always on the lookout for a better kitchen or a more lenient chef. They were of all ages, races, and birthplaces, and for the most part they worked in remarkable harmony. Theirs was a camaraderie born of shared struggle, respect for culinary craftsmanship, and a certain implied contempt for those who could never penetrate the mysteries of their calling. They referred to nonrestaurant types as "civilians," mere contemptibles who did not wear the starched, double-breasted chef jackets, the salad lady's baggy smock, or even the snap-buttoned cheap white dishwasher's shirt. Most had a particular animosity toward the customers, who, it was assumed, were in possession of way too much money and leisure time, while the kitchen crew worked their asses off for pitiful compensation. This sense of disentitlement provided many of them with an imagined excuse for their larcenous behavior. Others translated their frustrations into antisocial or personally destructive behavior patterns. All had fun doing so.

The single most important ingredient in successful kitchens is the ability of the staff to maintain a collective sense of humor. At that time, before any whiff of political correctness had entered the social lexicon, that tribal sense of humor took a rough form: pranks, hazing (that today would be termed harassment), and general silliness. Nicknames were ubiquitous. The broiler cook, a particularly zany individual, was "Squirrel." A waitress with rhinestoned glasses and frizzy hair was "Spaceship." A tall, thin, quiet cook with a formidable thirst was inexplicably known as "The Talking Stick." No one in the Ambassador kitchen sank to the nicknaming nadir of a neighboring restaurant, however, where the slow middle-aged female dishwasher was known simply as "Dipshit."

The tension in most restaurant kitchens is palpable. At any given moment there are dozens of deadlines occurring simultaneously for a multitude of workers crammed into a single large, hot, and very noisy room. The creation of edibles requires a series of unforgiving checkpoints in the progress of every dish for every table, every banquet, every meal cycle. The stress on individuals can be enormous, and laughter is oftentimes the only relief available to break the inherent tension. Sometimes, quips and banter are sufficient to lighten the mood. At other times spraying a fire extinguisher at a busy cook's backside or singing a profanity-laced lyric might do the trick. And for the abundantly endowed, there were the belly fights.

Our most prominent belly fighter was Tony Ficocello, who seemed to be working at the Ambassador only to fill his spare time. His main employment was procuring anything and everything for anyone in need. Want some Italian sausage? Tony produced it at home and could bring you what? Twenty pounds? Fifty? Just tell him when and where to deliver it. Fireworks? Guns? He had several pistols in the trunk of his car. Weed? Abortion pills or Spanish fly? Gambling? Tony would bring you to a craps game and drive you home when you were cleaned out. Girls? Well, he had to be careful because his wife didn't want him crossing into somebody else's "territory." Cryptic remarks like that intentionally led us to believe that Tony had ties to the Mafia, which we did not want to know any more about. This translated into special deals that Tony's clients quietly accepted without asking too many questions. When I went to buy my wedding rings from a jeweler that Tony recommended, the price immediately dropped $150 at the mere mention of his name. He was always genial toward the other workers in the Ambassador's kitchen, but that geniality was only genuine when directed at his fellow white males. Tony had nothing but ill-concealed contempt for anybody else. In that he was hardly unusual.

After all, the time was the late 1960s, and the traditional social order in America was breaking down, literally under fire. The news of the day was full of body counts from Vietnam, analysis of the generation gap separating young and old, and the first stirrings of feminist awareness and anger, and these issues could hardly be expected to remain outside the kitchen doors. Race relations were the most obvious fracture point, and even though the diverse crews in restaurant kitchens functioned harmoniously most of the time, suspicion and recrimination were not eradicated by the Great Society's efforts to bring about social justice. Riots in the black ghettoes in 1967 and 1968 only deepened the anxiety, especially among the predominantly poor whites working in service jobs. Their homes were frequently close to the neighborhoods in flames, and their instinctual response was often to parade their own ethnicities in order to counterbalance the newfound assertiveness of peoples of color. What everyone could agree on was, however, the remarkable upsurge in the availability and quality of street drugs in the aftermath of the riots. The consensus was that the government had called off the narcs in order to calm the inner city, and the crew at the Ambassador, regardless of color or creed, did its part in supporting the effort.

While Tony and others maintained their ethnicity as a badge of honor, others had their origins stamped on their passports and visas. Chef Logan had a penchant for hiring Europeans for kitchen positions, their main qualification being apparently that they, like him, were immigrants to the United States. Ferenc was a Hungarian who had fled Budapest two steps ahead of the Russian army in 1956. He maintained an uneasy truce with German Kurt the storekeeper, who sported a wooden hand, a souvenir of his service with the *Wehrmacht*. Kurt had lost his hand at Stalingrad, as he told it, and had then been invalided back to Germany, where he snagged the job of program director at Radio Berlin. This position seemed like awfully good fortune for a simple infantryman, and in subsequent conversations about his service in the Third Infantry Division, he mentioned dates and places that he remembered from his time on the Russian front. A little digging in the library revealed that mild-mannered, one-handed Kurt had actually served in the Third ss Division *Totenkopf,* a Nazi unit with a reputation for perpetrating atrocities wherever it happened to be marauding. In retrospect the loss of a hand was probably an insufficient penalty for Kurt's career of conquest, the radio job a sop to a wounded storm trooper with party connections. Kurt's only, very minor comeuppance came when Chef Logan held him personally responsible for the *Luftwaffe's* flattening of the East End of London during his boyhood.

The kitchen crew, like most others, was a model of diversity decades before anyone used the term or made money espousing it. All sorts, from ancient and thirsty Swiss sauté cooks to Ojibwe reservation refugees, punched the same time clock, mostly without punching each other. The most visible black cook was JohnnyT, the main breakfast cook in the coffee shop's open kitchen. JohnnyT was a prodigy. He could handle a busy breakfast rush of over three hundred customers without ever having any of the orders written down by the waitresses. The servers merely called out the multipart egg, omelet, and battered menu items they needed, and JohnnyT coolly, quickly, and accurately produced them all. He carried his own egg pans into work each day, and the skillets, his station, and even his jacket were impeccably clean at all times. He would also quietly sing Motown songs as he worked and keep up a stream of innuendo for the waitresses, just out of earshot of the customers. "C'mon to my house after work, baby. You know, the blacker the berry, the

sweeter the juice!" Or, "What do you mean, this is a 'rush order'? I'm not like your boyfriend; JohnnyT *always* takes his
time." Since breakfast cooks who can exert his kind of mastery were rare and, in this busy location, indispensable,
JohnnyT was respected, almost revered, by the other crew
members. The one person in the kitchen JohnnyT—or anybody else, for that matter—respected and deferred to was
Miss Del.

The setting for the Ambassador Motor Hotel's Sunday
brunch was the suburban spectacle of the Kashmiri Dining Room and the adjoining Shalimar Cocktail Lounge.
The space was decorated in what the motel's publicity bro-
chures described as "Regal Splendor," which meant lots of
draperies, fake carved sandalwood, and some large brass-
plated medallions hung haphazardly on the chintz-covered
walls. On the tables each purple water goblet weighed over
a pound; the china was stunning black on white; and real,
heavy sterling silverware glittered in profusion. Many former Ambassador employees retain complete sets of these
accoutrements to this day, having lovingly collected com-
pleter pieces one shift at a time. The most avid collectors,
the waitresses, were forced to wear cornflower blue dresses
with a crimson over-the-shoulder sash bordered with gold
braid. They looked like refugees from a high school production of *The King and I*.

Each Sunday, Oscar Husby and his extended family
proudly attended the Ambassador's Sunday brunch right after church. Because of the owner's fondness for the brunch,
the Ambassador's kitchen could not get away with saving the

week's leftovers and reworking them into a Sunday feast, as was and is the norm in far too many restaurants. Instead, everything was made fresh, especially the Scandinavian and Jewish selections on the cold-food side of the buffet. For this, large, shallow custom-made ice pans had been built that followed the kidney-shaped contours of the Shalimar's piano bar. On the ice were placed a couple dozen cold creations produced under the close supervision of Miss Del.

And now I too was under Miss Del's supervision. She taught me how to cook and grind chicken livers and form them into immense pâtés, how to fill circular molds with multihued gelatins, how to concoct composed salads to her precise specifications (I had to write down the ingredients, which she had cataloged in her memory), and how to peel, chop, and arrange huge volumes of fresh fruit to complement the frozen peaches and melon balls that completed the array. I learned to pipe softened butter to decorate whole smoked salmons, washed the slime off gefilte fish, and ran like a madman to refill and replace dishes as four to five hundred customers ravaged the display each week.

After a month Miss Del went to Chef Logan and informed him that henceforward she would be taking Sundays off because now Stevie (I've never allowed anybody else to call me "Stevie") would be able to handle the cold food. Why, he now knew as much as she did, and she would now be able to do the right thing on Sundays by going to church herself, and she might even include a prayer for his black Irish soul if she wasn't busy praying for those in greater need of Jesus's love. Inevitably, Chef Logan o-o-okayed her plan.

For the next two years Chef Logan arrived precisely at brunch-opening time, walked through the dining room to inspect the food, and went back to his office to do paperwork. Never once did he comment, positively or negatively, on the quality of the cold-food display.

The Triumph

The nineteenth century has been called the era of French international culinary hegemony. The diaspora of French kitchen talent that ensued from the exile of their aristocratic patrons during the Revolution sent some chefs into restaurants and others into foreign countries. These expatriates were soon followed by revolutionary and Napoleonic armies, in whose baggage trains traveled a coterie of skilled culinarians. Such service occasionally proved fatal. Joachim Murat, Napoleon's cavalry commander and brother-in-law, insisted on having his chef, Laguipiěre, included in his personal suite for the invasion of Russia. During the great retreat the old cook succumbed to the Russian winter, along with the heart of the Bonapartist delusion. French cuisine remained, however, victorious.

Despite two decades of incessant warfare during the Revolution and the empire, Paris and its restaurants flourished. Triumphs required celebration, either in the elaborate dining rooms of public restaurants or at grand spectacles in the palaces of the trumped-up new nobility. The newly enfranchised elite had risen from the bourgeoisie by luck or merit, and fine dining became the visible affirmation of their new-found status. The *nouveau riche* advertised their ascendancy by their choice of finer dining establishments. The emancipated class of chefs served both, sometimes simultaneously. As Napoleon established a new social order, fortunes rose and fell at his whim, and only a few of the new aristocrats had the time or money to re-create the private culinary establishments of the ancien régime. When a master chef's services were required, he was often borrowed from his own restaurant for the event. Without a doubt, the most celebrated of these double-duty chefs was Marie-Antoine Carême.

Befitting the plot of a romantic novel, Carême was born into an impoverished family of twenty-three children in 1784. At the age of ten, Carême was abandoned by his father at the gates of Paris, after being admonished to find a trade and make something of himself. Carême's chroniclers have frequently marveled at the serendipity that brought the lad into a caterer's premises and not those of a cobbler or a wheelwright. More likely than the hand of destiny, the pangs of hunger must have brought the young Carême into a humble cookshop, where he talked his way into an apprenticeship. He was a prodigy, and by the time he was sixteen, he had mastered his craft and applied to work for M. Bailly, the proprietor of the finest pastry shop in Paris.

Bailly recognized Carême's aptitude, as well as his drive to learn and perfect. Furthermore, Bailly saw that the young cook had a passion for architectural pastry creations, swirling towers of confectionary finesse that amazed and enchanted his fashionable customers, including the new first consul, General Bonaparte. Bailly encouraged Carême to study the architectural drawings in the national library, and thus inspired, Carême soon set the all-time standard for decorative *pieces montées* (sculptural confectionary center-pieces), creations that often graced the future emperor's table. A frequent guest at that table—and at every other significant table in Europe during the period—was the Marquis de Talleyrand.

The career of Charles Maurice de Talleyrand-Périgord is an inspiration to all those who seek to combine the blessings of longevity with the usefulness of treachery. Prior to the Revolution, his aristocratic, but somewhat penurious, family had secured a position for Talleyrand in the clergy—his clubfoot having kept him from pursuing a military career. By 1789, he had bribed and maneuvered his way through the ranks to become the bishop of Autun and was leading the church's fight for its ancient privileges as the storm gathered. With the fall of the Bastille, Talleyrand quickly and seamlessly changed sides, resigned his priesthood just before being excommunicated, and presided over the dismantling of the vast church property holdings throughout France. This ability to shift with whatever winds were blowing was the hallmark of Talleyrand's career. He served officially as minister, ambassador, and overall power broker in every French government—monarchy, convention, directory, republic, consulship, empire, and two restorations—until his death in 1834. In each employment he was implicated in seductions, intrigues, betrayals, assassinations, espionage, and embezzlements, all of which brought him great personal wealth, as well as a network of illicit connections that stretched from St. Petersburg to Washington, D.C. During Talleyrand's final break with Napoleon, at a time when Talleyrand was already selling French state secrets to the tsar of Russia, the emperor of Austria, and the king of England, the former general referred to the former bishop as "shit in a silk stocking." Talleyrand's reply: "Pity that so great a man should have been so ill-bred."

For Talleyrand a lack of breeding and good manners were the most dire human flaws, and throughout his long life he served as the arbiter of taste wherever his intrigues brought him. During the latter years of Napoleon's reign, Talleyrand remained the most influential person in France—though he was officially out of favor and banned from office—and one of the tools he used to maintain his influence was his talent for lavish dinners and entertainments. In support of this, he maintained a polished culinary establishment, and into that establishment he lured the greatest chef of the day, Marie-Antoine Carême. Setting off to the Congress of Vienna as a defeated France's ambassador, Talleyrand was accompanied by his diplomatic secret weapon, Carême. On that occasion he told the newly ensconced King Louis XVIII, "Sire, I have more need of casseroles than of written instructions." Carême's creations would accompany Talleyrand's machinations before the crowned heads of Europe.

Talleyrand had put Carême on an international stage. The congress was attended by the victorious European heads of state, who met to redraw national borders and redistribute the authority so recently scrambled by Napoleon and his armies. Talleyrand represented a beaten France that was a pariah among nations and a regicidal breaker of the status quo, and the other great powers aimed to have their revenge. In one of the most radical turnarounds in diplomatic history, Talleyrand managed, however, to play one conquering power against another, succeeding by bluff and intrigue, seduction and cajoling in revitalizing France's fortunes at the bargaining table. No huge indemnity was levied against the French, and the natural (i.e., prerevolutionary) frontiers of France were preserved. France emerged as an equal partner of those states who, before Talleyrand's diplomacy, were bent on humbling and dismembering her forever.

Many of the negotiations for rapprochement occurred at tables groaning under the products of Carême's genius. Carême's mastery of the culinary arts separated him from his predecessors in what one historian called a "seismic shift in the occupation itself," and his growing fame increasingly made him a symbol of France's resurgence and a valuable asset for her new rulers. So when Talleyrand wished to ingratiate himself and his government with Russia, he loaned Carême to Tsar Alexander for over a year. England's hedonistic prince regent was granted the great chef's services during his coronation festivities, and he also served the Baron de Rothschild. By this stage of his career, Carême was employed on retainer, however, journeying in his own carriage to the Rothschild estates only for special occasions. Rich and renowned, he had transcended any vestiges of the old patronage system, as Voltaire had in literature or Beethoven had in music. By the 1820s, Carême was a free agent, an acknowledged master, and the role model for every culinary practitioner in France. He had transformed the French menu, documented his creations in several comprehensive volumes, and established the role of chef as revolutionary autocrat, as well as chef as romantic hero, ennobled by his struggle. As he wrote in his memoir, *Le pâtissier royal parisien:*

> In this abyss of heat . . . the man in charge has to have a strong head, be focused on the task, and have the management skills of a great administrator. . . . He sees everything, he acts everywhere at once. . . . And is it to be believed? In this furnace everyone acts promptly, not a breath is heard; the Chef alone has a right to make himself heard, and everyone obeys his voice.

Chefs everywhere sought to emulate Carême, his cuisine, and, for better or worse, his omnipotence in the kitchen. After he died young in 1833—in the words of *Le grande dictionnaire de cuisine,* "killed by his own genius"—his legacy lived on, and everywhere cooks aspired to the pinnacle of French culinary practice, *haute cuisine.*

Haute Cuisine Crosses the Atlantic

The Delmonico brothers were two such aspirants. The elder, Giovanni Del-Monico, from Mairengo, Switzerland, had served as a sea captain until 1824. That year he became a landlubber, using his savings to open a wine shop near the

Battery in New York City. It failed. He returned to Switzerland to discover that his brother Pietro had become a successful confectioner in Berne. Pooling their resources, they decided to give the New World another try and relocated to New York. There they invested in a small café, which they intended to name Del-Monico and Brother. The sign painter misspelled their name, however, and delivered a sign that read "Delmonico." Rather than wait for a new one, the brothers simply changed their names, transforming themselves to "John" and "Peter" in the bargain. Assimilation takes many forms.

With Peter cooking and John working the front of the house, Delmonico's soon attracted a clientele of European émigrés who felt marooned in a land of barbarous food preparation. At that time American home cooking, at least along the Atlantic seaboard, was mostly a holdover from English cooking and thus was execrable. Away from home Americans had few food choices outside boardinghouses, with their rough fare, or saloons, where men could snack while getting drunk. At Delmonico's, native-born Americans gradually began to discover what their European neighbors were enjoying. Business boomed. By 1830, the brothers were forced to move to bigger quarters as customers flocked to enjoy the French-inspired fare and fine wines and, most of all, to see what a restaurant really was. Customers had the freedom to choose their repasts from an extensive menu while dining in an establishment dedicated solely to their comfort and satisfaction.

The restaurant grew steadily under the direction of the Delmonico family, moving to ever-larger buildings in more fashionable neighborhoods, acquiring a farm on Long Island for growing the best produce, and ultimately incorporating a luxury hotel, the finest in the city. When the family could no longer exert personal control over every aspect of the thriving business, they recruited an established chef from France, Charles Ranhofer, to oversee their kitchens. Arriving in 1862, Ranhofer was a kitchen despot in the mold of Carême; in fact his early career paralleled Carême's career closely, as did his talent and his attitude. In his memoir Lorenzo Delmonico, who hired Ranhofer, recounted his first meeting with the autocratic chef:

> He was perfect in dress and manner, and his attitude was such as to make me feel that he was doing me a great favor by coming into my employment. "You are the proprietor," he said. "Furnish the room and the provision, tell me the number of guests, and I will do the rest. . . . I am responsible and things must be done as I direct."

For the next three decades, Ranhofer held sway in the Delmonico's kitchen, becoming a celebrity in his own right, inventing an array of new dishes, and training the next generation of American chefs in the glories of French culinary practice. He cooked for presidents, visiting royalty, and the robber barons who presided over America's Gilded Age. So respected (and feared) was Ranhofer that one of his cooks, a victim of terminal despair, specifically exonerated his chef from blame in his suicide note. Almost single-handedly, Ranhofer made the French restaurant the model for all that was flavorful and sophisticated in American dining establishments. He also cemented the haughty, mercurial European chef as an archetype in American popular culture.

Drafted!

My weekend brunch creations kept me busy for a couple years, years in which I graduated from high school and enrolled at the University of Minnesota. I imagined that a college education would be my passport out of kitchen service. Moreover, it supplied me with a nifty student draft deferment, which guaranteed that the only uniform I'd need to worry about was white. It was 1968, and the world was plainly going to hell. New casualty lists appeared in the newspaper every day, alongside accounts of urban violence, drug addiction, and annoying hippies with too much time on their hands. White people classified themselves in a number of ways: hawks or doves, rednecks or heads, boozers or users. Beatles or Stones? Humphrey or McCarthy? *Nixon?*

Meanwhile, the black employees at the Ambassador had a nervous, haunted look as their neighborhoods burned while they were away serving white people in St. Louis Park. Only my friend JohnnyT, the breakfast cook, remained stalwartly calm. We all knew that most of his serenity was chemically induced, but his cheery demeanor was always welcomed. Life was never so serious that JohnnyT took it seriously. He was his own man, never prone to drama or anger, and we gravitated toward each other because we shared an outsider status. I was a white boy doing black women's work, and JohnnyT referred to himself as "the fly in the buttermilk" of the all-white coffee shop.

On summer break from college, I cadged a few extra hours at the Ambassador, prepping food for the brunch or helping out wherever needed. The work wasn't demanding, but it put gas in my car and allowed me to save up some tuition money. One afternoon, Chef Logan came out of his office and walked over to where I was working.

"Mister fucking s-s-student, I need you to be here at 5:30 tomorrow morning."

I was about to protest the early, unanticipated start time when I realized that the chef had tears welling up in his dark eyes. Clearly, all it was prudent to ask was why.

"I just got a ph-phone call. JohnnyT got into a car wreck a few hours ago. He's dead, son. And I need a breakfast cook tomorrow. Shit!"

The chef left before anyone could see him crying.

Fish Eye

Out here in the Flatlands, a thousand miles from any salt-water other than sauerkraut brine, the restaurant's repertoire of seafood dishes tended to be thin. Since only frozen fish were generally available, most chefs found that their greatest challenge in preparing ocean fish was in camouflaging their mediocre taste and gummy texture. Lobster tails had to be drowned in butter; shrimp had to be breaded and fried until they curled up on themselves like briny doughnuts whose crumbly coating at least held a gooey tartar sauce all the way to the diner's maw. We won't even address the millions of bricks of frozen cod that quivered under a blanket of starchy cream sauce, except to mention that the name of the dish—*torsk!*—was also the sound that a slab of the stuff made when it dropped into your unsuspecting stomach.

My very favorite preparation, at least at the Ambassador, was something we called Dover Sole Waleska. In order to create this delicacy, the cook took a whole flat fish, frozen hard as a shingle, and thawed its exterior under cold running water. The skin could then be pulled off with a mighty tug, exposing the rigid flesh from mouth to tail. A knife was inserted along either side of the unfortunate creature's spine, and enough meat was peeled back to form the lips of a four-inch pocket that Georgia O'Keefe—and every cook—could appreciate. The whole thing was then covered in breadcrumbs and deep-fried. After the sole's final swim, the aforementioned gash was filled with that same starchy cream sauce and augmented with tomato paste and thawed crabmeat.

Onto a platter it went, with some lemon wedges, and out to the dining room. There the server struggled tableside to deconstruct this mess and convey it to the salivating guest's plate. The thought that fishermen on a roiling ocean risked their lives in order to secure the makings for a Waleska is troubling.

Things around the Twin Cities improved dramatically in 1981. That year a young Chicago native named Suzanne Weinstein moved to Minneapolis, determined to open a business of her own. Using contacts she had from a previous job, Suzanne arranged for some New Jersey fishermen to pack some of their catch in shaved ice and ship it overnight to the local airport. Her first consignment was a very large, very ugly tilefish, which she picked up and drove to a Chinese grocery that had a little extra cooler space. Before the day was over, Suzanne had sold the oddity to a local chef. It was the beginning of a multimillion-dollar business called Coastal Seafoods.

In very short order, every nice restaurant in town was featuring Coastal's fresh fish on its menu. Groupers and bluefish, sea bass and halibuts, snappers and swordfish were suddenly everywhere. Chefs like me would simply call Suzanne to see what was available that day and place their orders. She hustled and provided great service, initially as a one-person operation. The rented cooler gave way to a small warehouse; the car was followed by a refrigerated van. She found herself competing with long-established purveyors whose be-suited salespeople were appalled when Suzanne showed up ahead of them in various restaurant offices, reeking of fish and wearing fatigue pants and a T-shirt with the message "Welcome Visitors from Other Planets."

As frozen fish became passé here in the heartland, kitchen personnel had to learn the ways of fresh-fish cookery, so different and demanding. Even butchering fresh fish is an art, as so much care is needed to avoid bruising the delicate flesh. Luckily, the structure of these creatures is fairly simple, befitting their station on the food chain. A prehistoric thing like a sturgeon, all studded with knots of bony armor, can mightily resist the efforts of the boning knife, however, even in far more skillful hands than my own. Still, I think I've dismembered nearly every common piscine species at least once.

A trip to Boston confirmed this. While there, I was shanghaied into a visit to the venerable New England Aquarium, perhaps the dullest place in a city replete with run-down, dull attractions. The aquarium was one of the first built with the aim of making the visitor fear carp. Instead of majestically gazing down upon the lower forms, the visitor walked into an area where he was literally surrounded by tanks of cavorting sea creatures, all close by and at eye level. The effect was stunning because the viewer immediately felt like a sponge or a shrimp besieged by teeming shoals of oceanic denizens. What's worse, upon stepping into the midst of the swimming mass, I realized that a great many of their close relatives had been mutilated by my knives. Scads of scrod and every other finny thing cruised by, their frowning mouths and bulging, unblinking eyes giving the impression of their silently and eerily forming the syllables "j'accuse!" Only a thin pane of aquarium glass separated me from their cold-blooded re-venge. The hair stood up on my neck, and I retreated quickly. That night I had dinner at the Union Oyster House, secure in knowing that none of the mollusks there would be giving me the evil eye.

4

Plat Principal

Debacle at Dawn

To tell the truth, I had cooked breakfast before. When things were slow, I had occasionally taken over from JohnnyT when he went on break or called a girl. I also had the cocky attitude that went along with service in the Ambassador's kitchen. How hard could cooking breakfast be? After all, I had fed far more customers at brunch than I was likely to see during a single shift in the coffee shop. I set the station up doubly well before going home the night before: plenty of pancake batter and French toast batter and lots of omelet garnish. I needed to do well for JohnnyT—I knew he'd want it that way— and more important, I needed to show Chef Logan that I was more than just a pantry-boy relief cook. I was smart enough to work this station. After all, I was in college, and only a handful of the other cooks had even finished high school.

Having barely slept the night before, I got in early to put the final touches on my setup. I brought a full case of eggs out of the cooler and stacked the cardboard flats next to my grill. I filled a pitcher with ice water and stashed it under the counter so that I wouldn't need to step away even if I got thirsty. I stashed a pack of cigarettes in the waitress station so that I would be just five feet away from a smoke if I needed to steady myself. I was ready. My first moment of panic came when I realized I hadn't turned on the griddle, but it was early so—click—no harm done. Then I felt around the storage shelf for some egg skillets and came up with not JohnnyT's immaculate pans but some neglected, charred, scarred, and despicable-looking egg pans that had clearly seen better days. Second moment of panic.

By then the waitresses were trundling in, having heard through their grapevine that JohnnyT had shuffled off this mortal coil, and clearly some were heartbroken. Others were visibly angry at JohnnyT for having been so reckless and, oddly, at me for not being JohnnyT. I thought I had said all the right things about mourning, persevering, and going easy on the new guy, probably emphasizing the new guy part. My partner on the breakfast line came in. Her name was Willa Mae, and she and JohnnyT had been close. Her eyes were red, and she seemed pretty shaky, until she saw me. Then she was shaking. Willie Mae had never particularly liked me, this white college boy, and now that she was stuck out here with me, she was, as near as I could tell, somewhere between irritated and enraged. Obviously, I'd get no help from Willa Mae.

The hostess arrived and unlocked the front door. She was an older lady who had been a waitress for years before her arches broke down and forced her into a less-demanding role. Her job now was to greet customers, distribute them evenly in each of the five waitresses' stations, and offer departing diners a mint as they paid their checks. She also had to answer the phones, keep the front of the coffee shop tidy, and, hardest of all, be pleasant to each member of the Ambassador's management as they came in to cadge a free breakfast. She was rather selective as to which fools she would suffer gladly. I don't think I was one of them.

The bakery guy arrived. Every morning he'd show up with two long, flat heavy-gauge cardboard boxes of assorted doughnuts and danish for the Ambassador's breakfast service. This was a much-anticipated delivery, as all the employees with a sweet tooth (mainly due to substance abuse) crowded around to grab their favorite pastries. The delivery guy, as usual, admonished the breakfast cook, me today, to make sure that the empty bakery boxes were given to Paul, one of the main kitchen cooks. Paul had been designated to put those boxes aside for the deliveryman to pick up a few hours later. The idea was that, since the boxes themselves were expensive, the Ambassador could keep its bakery costs down by preserving them for reuse. The reality was that Paul would surreptitiously fill those boxes with beef tenderloins, sirloins, or lobster tails and put them aside. The deliveryman returned and picked them up later, thanking everyone for their thriftiness, and then met Paul after his shift to divide up the loot.

So we were ready for business.

The first customers arrived, were seated, and ordered their food. "A waffle and two eggs scrambled," the waitress called. Good. Willa Mae worked the waffle iron, and scrambled eggs were easy. I cracked two eggs into a pan, doing the *very* professional one-handed egg crack, nonchalantly flipped the shells into the garbage can, and swirled my fork into the pan, well and truly scrambling the eggs. They cooked quickly, perhaps too quickly. As I poured the cooked eggs onto the plate, I noticed that Willa Mae had just started the waffle. Worse, there was a lot of scrambled egg cooked solidly, immovably, to the sides and bottom of the pan. Obviously, this pan was pitted and hadn't been seasoned, the long process whereby a pound of salt is heated up with oil in the pan, the salt acting as an abrasive to smooth the surface of the skillet's metal. I tossed it aside. Oh well, I still had five pans left—for the moment.

Since the waffle took forever in the lukewarm iron, by the time it was finished the scrambled eggs were stone cold, and the waitress rightly demanded a replacement. No problem, except the second pan duplicated the performance of the first, only more so. The restaurant was filling up now, with the waitresses scurrying about with coffee and juice and writing down orders at each table. We were getting slammed. They were soon shouting things that sounded like TWOEGGSBASTEDWITHASIDEOFHASHBROWNSANDBACONE XTRACRISPYUPWITHTWOPOACHEDFIRMONTOPOFASHORTSTACK.

HOWSOONONTHATCHEESEOMELET? Oh, the cheese omelet! The one I put in the oven a few minutes ago. I'll just open the five-hundred-degree oven and quickly grab it and AHHHH! SON OF A BITCH, FUCKIN' A!!! Hot plate. I plunged my seared hand into my carefully prepared ice water.

By now all five waitresses were standing across the counter from me, screaming orders and begging for the food they had ordered seemingly hours ago. Yolks were breaking, and whites were singeing. My pans were still sticking badly, so I adopted the expedient of just loading them with oil before dropping in the eggs. Basically, I was deep-frying every order, and the eggs slid across the plates in a queasy puddle of vegetable oil. I fantasized about JohnnyT in his coffin, with his hands curled around those pristine skillets of his, as neglected pancakes blackened and I tried to figure out which omelet was filled with what.

By this time I had asked the waitresses to write their orders down, as I clearly could not remember what anybody needed. This annoyed them even more, but they each took a place mat, put their name on top, and began writing out their orders, each in a different and mutually unintelligible shorthand. All except for one. The new girl from Tennessee was standing in front of me, wide-eyed and trying to make sense of a fistful of guest checks. Her hands were shaking, and occasionally a check would escape her fingers and float to the greasy floor. Looking out from the open kitchen, I could see scowling customers staring at me or trying to flag down their harried servers. Glancing back, Tennessee girl was now openly sobbing, her shoulders heaving as she buried her head in her hands across the pickup counter. A meltdown. Her guest checks were scattered everywhere, and the other waitresses just maneuvered around her in a frantic effort to get what little food was coming up out to their customers.

Enough guests had now walked out or refused to pay that the hostess came over and added her raspy voice to the general din. Willa Mae disgustedly slammed her butter spreader down and walked off the coffee shop line and into the main kitchen. I was eyeing the exit too, seriously contemplating the ignominy of walking out, defeated and grievously incompetent, when two veteran cooks appeared from the main kitchen and elbowed me aside. They calmed the waitresses, cleared the debris from my station, and manfully set about making things right in the coffee shop. It probably took us an hour to reestablish order and feed the remaining customers. This debacle had cost the waitresses some serious tip money, but the refugee from Tennessee had disappeared, apparently forever, and all agreed that she wouldn't be missed. Finally, the servers turned their anger toward Chef Logan, who had obviously put me out there under fire with no effort to train me on the breakfast station. It was he who showed up next.

By the time I saw him, he had already been briefed by some of the jeering cooks, and he was plainly angry. Having listened too much to the newly sympathetic waitresses, I was now full of what felt like righteous indignation myself. I had experienced quite enough humiliation for one day.

*   *   *

The Milieu

The French culinary evangelism that spread throughout the Europe-dominated world in the nineteenth century has always been written about in terms of its greatest proselytizers. We have already made the acquaintance of Carême and Ranhofer, who stand in for hundreds of other capable chefs of this period, and we will soon meet the greatest of them all. None of these notable names would have come down to us had they been merely autodidacts exercising their genius in private and not marshaling the forces under their command. We seldom hear about those supporting forces. Generation after generation of anonymous *commis* (apprentices), *pâtissiers* (pastry cooks), *chefs de partie* (line cooks), and lowly *plongeurs* (dishwashers) made the careers of the great chefs possible. The passion and toil of these workers, as well as their subservience, were the currency chefs spent to buy notoriety.

Theirs was a realm existing, both literally and figuratively, underground. Kitchens of restaurants and hotels in major cities were located in windowless basements. In an era before mechanical ventilation, air entered through holes at pavement level, though they were often filled to prevent the egress of obnoxious odors or the ingress of vermin. The heat generated by the kitchen's ovens, grills, and rotisseries therefore mostly stayed in the kitchen, along with some of the smoke and the fumes from the various appliances. Gaslights sputtering to give some weak light only added to the inferno, and even the doors opening to other sections of the establishment had to be kept tightly closed during meal periods to prevent drafts from cooling food destined for the customers. The floors were covered with greasy sawdust, and an ember falling from a charcoal-fired rotisserie could easily set the shavings afire.

The introduction of cast-iron cookers at midcentury did little to alleviate the hellish atmosphere. These great stoves, roughly twenty feet long and ten to twenty feet wide, dominated the center of the kitchen. Each morning the crew's apprentices would load the stove with coal and get it burning in time for the cooks to work around its perimeter. The flue pipes of the great stoves often leaked and vented poisonous fumes directly into the workspace. The fires within were stoked throughout the day, and the thick iron plates glowed under the pots and pans as the cooks prepared the complicated, multifarious menus of the time. Those pots and pans, when dirty, were stacked up in the corners of the kitchen, awaiting the eventual attention of the plongeurs, who typically suffered the loss of all their fingernails from the continual scraping and scrubbing. Open drains carried waste water away but often became plugged, flooding the kitchen and adding to the general misery.

Years of working in these conditions inevitably took a toll on the health of the cooks. Their afflictions included slow asphyxiation from the fumes of the cooking appliances, tuberculosis, undernourishment, varicose veins from standing throughout long shifts, and deformations of the ankle from carrying heavy loads. An 1883 article in *La Revue de l'Art Culinaire* reported that most cooks died in their early forties and that there were more occupational diseases to be found among cooks than among miners. The greatest scourge for the cooks was, however, chronic alcoholism. Sweating profusely in these infernal regions, cooks sucked down whatever beer, wine, or spirits they could find, and sauciers making wine- or liquor-based concoctions were the most prone to abusing the ingredients. Most of the ordinary cooks toiled on in a more or less continual stupor until they died. Only the most astute or ambitious made it out of the restaurant kitchens to private service or the exalted status of head chef. Even Carême himself lived to be only fifty, succumbing too young to his early years of drudgery.

This stultifying atmosphere had little to recommend it, and those uninitiated into its sweltering precincts had little desire to visit. Besides, the cooks who populated the kitchens had a reputation as uncouth, vulgar, and occasionally violent. Shouted obscenities as well as crashing crockery could often be heard by restaurant diners, and the chefs' purported bullying of their staffs, with frequent resort to corporal punishment, seemed eminently justifiable to the public. The cooks themselves called their chosen employment le métier (the profession) and were largely fatalistic about its outcome.

A young man gained entry to this fiery underworld through an apprenticeship, a system that was in itself brutalizing. Parents would deliver their thirteen-year-old son to a chef-patron and pay a fee to feed, house, and train the young man for a period of three years. The apprentice had to supply his own clothing, shoes, aprons, hats, and even bedding. During apprenticeship the boy was supposed to live in a dormitory, but few proprietors actually could afford such accommodations. In reality the apprentice often slept in a corner of the kitchen or in the stables with the horses. Essentially, his parents had purchased the youth three years of slavery.

The apprentice's day started early, as he accompanied his master to the market to procure provisions for the day's meal service. These he had to carry back to the restaurant across the crowded pavements, either on his head or in an overloaded wheelbarrow. The rest of the day and evening was consumed with menial tasks and periodic abuse from workers with more seniority or skill. Often he was bullied mercilessly by his coworkers, and it was common for chefs to mete out rough treatment, including kicks and blows, to the newcomer. Formal training barely existed, and the young man learned by observing experienced crew members on the job. The apprentice could be discharged for any reason, without compensation, and new employers seldom opened their doors to those who failed elsewhere. Anyone who succeeded in this gauntlet of abuse had to prove himself daily, in order to graduate to the status of *commi,* the lowest order of kitchen worker in the fiery world of le métier.

Escoffier

The man almost singularly responsible for civilizing the restaurant kitchen was Auguste Escoffier. He had the good fortune of being born near Nice in 1846, far from the pressure cooker of the Paris restaurant milieu. Although he went through the normal process of culinary apprenticeship, the circumstances were mitigated by his uncle's owning the establishment. The restaurant offered delivery to every address in Nice, then as now a fashionable resort destination on the Mediterranean. One of the apprentice's duties was making these deliveries, and so the young Escoffier gained admittance to the sumptuous residences along the Côte d'Or. Inside, he observed everything and recorded for future reference his impressions of clothes, table settings, styles of service, manners, and expressions. His uncle also favored the boy by putting him in charge of procurement for the restaurant. This gave him access to produce from Provence, seafood from the Mediterranean, and meat and game from Piedmont. Few regions on earth are better situated for sourcing an abundance of gustatory delights.

Escoffier was an apt pupil, learning every station in the restaurant's kitchen and nearly every technique practiced in the provincial establishment. He astonished his peers with his expertise, and all realized that Nice was too small a stage for his art. Like all promising cooks, he aspired to a position in Paris. Completing his apprenticeship, he applied for a position at Le Petit Moulin Rouge and began working at that famous location in 1865. His first job was as rôtisseur, in charge of all the roasted meats and fish on the menu. In addition, he was responsible for soufflés and deep-fried items. This meant that each day he simultaneously labored over charcoal grills, open-fired rotisseries, and sputtering vats of fat, running to and fro in the barely organized kitchen.

After a couple years of this, Escoffier was promoted to the *garde manger* (cold-food cook) and then saucier positions, a phenomenal rise in less than five years.

Paris in those years was truly the capital of the world. Another Bonaparte, Louis Napoleon, reigned as Emperor Napoleon III. The city itself was being redesigned at his behest, the broad boulevards and monuments we know today replacing the ancient warrens of the city. It was La Ville-lumière (The City of Lights), the intellectual, political, and cultural beacon of Europe, and visitors flocked to Paris from all corners of the globe. One of its undoubted attractions was the haute cuisine available in its restaurants, setting the standard for fine dining everywhere. Le Petit Moulin Rouge was one of its brightest lights, and Auguste Escoffier was rising inexorably as one of its most inspired and skillful contributors.

The officer corps of the French army continued to show its good taste by requiring accomplished chefs to accompany the headquarters on campaign. When the Franco-Prussian War broke out in 1870, Escoffier was still serving in the reserves and was mobilized and sent to the front to feed the generals. These generals, it turned out, were much abler at gourmandizing than they were at strategizing, and France was quickly and utterly defeated. Escoffier was nearly killed on several occasions, but in the end he trudged off to a prisoner of war camp when most of the army surrendered. Even in captivity, however, the French general staff had its privileges, and Escoffier finished out his confinement in tolerable comfort serving the defeated officers.

In a sense Escoffier's capture had been a stroke of luck. Had he remained in Paris, he would have undoubtedly undergone the horrors of the siege the Prussian army conducted against the capital. The population was reduced to starvation as German shells rained on the city. Most of the restaurants closed for want of provisions, though some kept going by offering meals of cat, dog, or rat. Even the animals in the zoo were slaughtered, and for a few days those who could afford it dined on elephant or ocelot. Instead of enduring these privations, Escoffier was imprisoned hundreds of miles away, with plenty of time for thinking.

His experience in the army, though decidedly unsatisfactory, had taught him a lot about organization. Escoffier began to imagine a wholesale redesign of the kitchen staff, where each worker would have separate and distinct duties that followed a rigid chain of command. He termed this the brigade system, and it is still in use today in nearly every restaurant worthy of the name. As expediency forced Escoffier to shorten ingredient lists and reengineer courses, he came to realize that the menus of the time, largely imitations of Carême's practices from decades ago, were too lengthy and complicated. Experiencing real hunger for the first time as a captive, Escoffier realized that foods themselves, not ritual and embellishment, were what brought people to the table. Finally, Escoffier concluded that captivity in a squalid military prison was not all that different from working in the restaurant kitchens of the time, and he set out to change things. After his liberation these ideas drove Escoffier to action for the rest of his long career. He summed this up in his autobiography:

Having realized that there was, in the field of cooking, a vast domain to explore and develop, I said to myself, "Even though this is not the [circumstance] I personally would have chosen, since I am here, let me work to make the grade and do my best to improve the standing of the kitchen chef." This has always been my goal, and I think I have given ample proof of my devotion to this cause.

Escoffier returned to the milieu more determined than ever. In 1878, he opened his first restaurant, Le Faisan d'Or, in Cannes. Moving on to Monte Carlo, he took over the kitchens of the Grand Hotel, making it a world culinary destination. Escoffier's visionary cooking and dedication to quality soon made him famous, as did his writings. A superb organizer, he also popularized his theories on running a successful operation. These included modernization of kitchen design to make facilities more healthful and holding cooks to a higher standard of performance and deportment. Foul language was banned from Escoffier's kitchens, as was sloppy appearance and poor hygiene. Moreover, this greatest of chefs advocated for culinarians to have formal education, health care, and even treatment for alcoholism. His goal was nothing less than to make his profession respectable.

During the summer season Escoffier also ran the kitchen operation of the Hotel National in Lucerne. There he met César Ritz, the great hotelier. They formed a partnership and, in 1890, moved to the Savoy Hotel in London, where they established the model for the back-of-the-house and front-of-the-house operational modes that continue to this day. Successful on every level, they gained control of many of the finest establishments of the day, started the Ritz Hotel chain, and established Escoffier as the acknowledged master of international haute cuisine. Training under Escoffier was the surest route to success. At the Ritz Carlton in London, he trained a pastry chef by the name of Ho Chi Minh, who really never lived up to his potential as a pâtissier. Later in life, Escoffier settled down to catalog all the recipes of fine French cooking, including his own numerous contributions. He also edited culinary journals and wrote his memoirs, in which he conveniently forgot to mention that both he and Ritz had been fired from the Savoy for accepting kickbacks from suppliers.

Showdown

My conversation with Chef Logan in the aftermath of the breakfast disaster was conducted, at least initially, at a high decibel level. Retelling it verbatim would be impossible, both because my memory is not all that exact and because my sputtering was answered with Logan's stuttering and the resultant dialog would be much too long and difficult to punctuate. Here's the gist of it.

Righteous indignation was the only card I held, and I played it early.

"Why wasn't I given any training before being thrown to the wolves on the breakfast station?"

"Why should I bother training the likes of *you?*"

"What's the matter with *me?*"

"Well, for one thing, you're a waste of my time. You'll be gone soon, and I'll just have to train somebody else."

"Are you firing me?"

"Not really. All I'm saying is that once you're done with fucking school, you'll be gone like every other educated idjit. It's all just a part-time job for you, so you can afford beer and pussy. You've got no dedication. You only want to learn what you need to get by. I hope the university teaches you something, because you're not learning shit here."

Weakening now.

"Well . . . maybe if I had a better teacher."

"Look son, I've taught certifiable retards to be better cooks than you'll ever be. At the Savoy Hotel I had to train a crew of bleedin' Pakistanis. I can teach anybody, except for people who have been to cooking school. They're hopeless. I could even teach a . . . What are you studying in college?"

"Ah . . . political science."

"Well, I think I could teach even a political fucking scientist if he was willing to learn."

"Dammit, I want to learn! And I'm not an idjit just because I go to school . . . "

But there it was. The kitchen culture had a deep suspicion of formal education of every sort. In the world of culinary professionals, on-the-job training was viewed as the sole legitimate path to career success. Most of the cooks had barely finished high school, while many, including the chef, had never graduated at all. Though some occasionally expressed regret about their lack of schooling, most felt that wasting any additional time in the classroom would only have cost them money later on. Better to work, earn, and learn than to sit through hours of some boring sod trying to explain algebra or, in my own case, Latin.

Paul replaced me the next day on the breakfast station. This meant that I could go to JohnnyT's funeral at the old Baptist church in North Minneapolis. Ambassador employees were the only white people in attendance, and I found myself sitting next to Chef Logan during the service. Afterward, he invited me to have a beer with him, but there was no such thing as *a* beer in Logan's world. We went to a bar where being underage was nullified by being with John Logan. The hours in the bar sped by, and I woke up the next morning, pried my eyes open, and prayed for death. When my prayers went unanswered, I got dressed and went to work. Logan was already there, in fine spirits, and when I walked in, he said, "About f-f-fucking time you got here. Let's get started."

Apparently, we had resumed our discussion at the bar after the funeral and had come to some sort of understanding, the details of which I probably forgot during my fourteenth trip to the restroom. At any rate, I must have promised to get serious about my work, and for his part Chef Logan had decided to try to give me a real education. True to my principles, I never wavered in my determination to excel in college. Having started at the university in 1967, I finished my course work in 1981 and walked down the aisle in cap and gown in 1995 to receive my political science bachelor's, with a soaring GPA of 2.56. But the eight years following our postfuneral binge was when I really got educated. Chef Logan put me in every situation in his kitchen where I could learn. I worked every station under his guidance, helped in culinary competitions, baked thousands of the infamous loaves of soda bread for various Irish festivals, and even got involved in union politics as an election judge and contract negotiator. When he bought an Irish bar downtown, Logan had me do the cooking. When he agreed to cater an out-of-town wedding, I was the one who had to drive the stolen supplies to the site in my *(shudder)* Gremlin, while he flew down in a borrowed private plane. After ten years at the Ambassador, I was the sous-chef, the number-two man in the Ambassador's kitchen, the chef's protégé.

So I found it surprising when Chef Logan sat down with me in his office and informed me that I would soon be leaving the Ambassador. He had concluded, correctly, that there was nothing left for me to learn at the Island in the Sun and that I needed to move on as the next step in my career. Before I could ask where I would go, he announced that he had spoken to the chef at the Sheraton Ritz Hotel in downtown Minneapolis and that I would be starting in this much larger, much more complex property in two weeks as sous-chef. It was all arranged, even my minimal pay raise. Naturally, I was shocked, but by this point I was showing some restlessness, and Logan clearly thought I was ready to take the next step. How could I argue with *him?*

On my last day at the Ambassador, Logan approached me, wished me luck, and promised to help me in any way, blah, blah, blah. I thanked him, and he handed me something, saying, "You might n-n-need this." It was a tattered little book, grease-stained and dog-eared, that had plainly seen more than a few years' service in kitchens. The book was Chef Logan's own copy of *Le repertoire de la cuisine* by Auguste Escoffier.

Tequila Turkey

Ingredients

1 fresh tom turkey, 16 to 18 lbs

1 tbsp pepper

1 tbsp salt, plus one nearly empty box of salt (iodized OK)

2 to 3 bottles (or maybe more, who knows?) inexpensive tequila

1 dozen lemons, hacked into wedges

4 to 6 friends, preferably college students, reprobates, or any combination of the two

Preparation

1. On a Saturday afternoon at work, be reminded that to-morrow morning the chef will be appearing on his weekly television show.

2. Familiarize yourself with the turkey now safely chilling in the walk-in cooler. Understand that since it is nearly Thanksgiving, the chef desires to demonstrate the proper technique for carving the festive bird for his enraptured TV audience.

3. Promise the chef that you will come in early on Sunday morning in order to give the turkey plenty of time to roast. Further, promise him that the turkey will have a

luscious appearance so that everyone at home will believe that only a REAL CHEF could have produced something looking so delicious.

4. Upon arriving at your firetrap off-campus student rental dump, discover that there is already a party in progress. Observe that the revelers are doing the classic, I-saw-it-in-a-movie tequila ritual. Become intrigued.

5. Sprinkle some salt into the little hollow where your thumb meets the back of your hand, and then place a hacked lemon wedge between that selfsame thumb and your index figure. With your free hand, pour yourself a shot of inexpensive tequila.

6. In quick succession, lick the salt, knock back the tequila, and suck on the lemon. Note: At this point you should be hearing slurred shouts of manly approval and encouragement from your colleagues.

7. Repeat twenty-six times. Note: This is an approximation based on outcome. Your results may vary.

8. Sleep.

9. Awaken to find your head being massaged by a pile driver. Discover that the main sewer in Guadalajara has somehow been diverted through your mouth. Worse, notice that it is already 8:00 AM. Panic.

10. With one eye open, drive recklessly to work. Upon arrival, retch deeply when first encountering odor of food; then run to turn on oven. Set oven to 550°F. Run to cooler to find turkey. Note: At this point your face should be the same color as the skin of the raw turkey.

11. Place turkey in roasting pan, and throw it into the oven, acting nonchalant as coworkers inquire as to why you're so late and why your face is the color of a raw turkey. Explain as necessary.

12. Periodically (perhaps every 4½ minutes), peer into oven and realize that the turkey is barely changing color. Be sure that a wave of nausea washes over you each time as the heat and the realization hit you squarely in the forehead. Imagine yourself seeking employment in a sheltered workshop after the chef has inflicted traumatic bodily injury upon you. Compulsively check time. Think.

13. Brush the turkey with melted butter. Wait the customary 4½ minutes. Repeat.

14. Brush the turkey with Kitchen Bouquet caramel coloring. Notice that the dark brown gunk gives you a brief flicker of hope.

15. Just before the chef is due to arrive, remove turkey from oven and jam the whole thing under a 1,500°F infrared broiler. Watch carefully as blast of concentrated heat

turns the top of the thing a deep, rich golden brown. Remove from broiler as the chef enters and begins bellowing for his turkey, as he too is running late.

16. Remove turkey from pan and wrap in aluminum foil. Hold breath as the chef peels back a corner of the foil and grunts in satisfaction. Convey turkey to the chef's car. Begin doing the other nine hundred tasks you've neglected in order to prepare turkey for television.

17. At 11:30 AM, ignore remaining duties and go to bar. Turn TV to proper channel just as program hostess is yammering on about the wonders of the holidays and introducing the chef and his perfectly browned little friend. Ignore audio as camera focuses on turkey, resting on a white cutting board. Notice that some sort of dark liquid is puddling under the bird. Feel a return of extreme queasiness.

18. Observe as camera focuses extreme close-up and the chef begins demonstrating proper carving technique. Shudder as carving knife encounters visible resistance to first cut but then is forcefully plunged deep into turkey to separate thigh and drumstick. Sicken as bright red gout of grade A turkey blood gushes from incision and spreads across white cutting board in a display of carnage unequalled on live TV since the demise of Lee Harvey Oswald. Barely hear the stammered excuses as camera hurriedly focuses elsewhere. Break out in a cold sweat.

19. Await return of the chef while perusing help-wanted ads in Sunday paper. Endure tongue lashing that somehow ends in smile on the chef's face as he mentions that obnoxious crew in TV studio (whom the chef hates anyway) devoured semiraw turkey after end of program. Speculate jointly on their inevitable gastric distress.

20. Swear off tequila forever.

5

Salade

Detour

The five years following my departure from the Ambassador Motor Hotel take up an inordinate number of lines on my résumé. After a relatively stable decade of work and school, and work and work, I found myself suddenly exploring the job market, or most of it anyway. My tenure as sous-chef of the Sheraton Ritz Hotel lasted less than six months. The chef and I never hit it off, the hours were long, and the salary was short at a hotel that I belatedly learned was a money-losing tax shelter for the Sheraton corporation and already slated for demolition. Moreover, the day I gave my notice, I learned that two of the cooks I supposedly was supervising were in cahoots with a Sikh waiter in the hotel's posh dining room.

Each night, groups of the waiter's Indian friends would dine extravagantly in our restaurant. Their food was prepared by my cooks off the books in consideration for the drinks and drugs forwarded to them by the Sikh. They were all three apprehended the day after I left and summarily fired. Fortunately, when confronted, they told the management that I had known nothing about their scam.

From there I sought out another kitchen management position and found one working for the Canteen Corporation. Canteen, a food service contractor, ran the dining facility at the Minneapolis Federal Reserve Bank. Their chef had suffered a heart attack and was not expected to recover, so the management was happy to find that I was immediately available. I went to work doing some supervision but mostly preparing elaborate meals for the bank's officers in their executive dining room. They could afford them, sitting as they were on top of limitless piles of money. I was reminded of this each morning when I reported for work and announced myself at the building's intercom, which was squarely in the sights of a machine gun. Nevertheless, it was a nice situation for me: new kitchen, fine ingredients, compliant management. The fact that I was basically a mediocre cook went all but unnoticed. And then a miracle occurred.

The old chef was rejected by the angels, recovered, and wanted to come back to work. Canteen now faced the dilemma of what to do with me. Since I seemed capable enough and tended to show up when I was scheduled, they decided that a promotion was in order. They announced that I would receive a raise and be assigned to one of their

biggest accounts. I became the chef at the Ford plant in
St. Paul. As prestigious as that may sound, the reality of
the situation was less than ideal. The workers at the plant
were mostly long-term autoworkers who were repeatedly
spooked by personnel layoffs, which occurred regularly during the Carter recessions and oil crises. They wanted meat
(of no particular derivation) and potatoes (instant mashed,
instant gravy) and no bullshit. I tried to give them all three
in a kitchen that Henry Ford had value-engineered in 1921,
a kitchen that would flood almost daily, with a weak ventilation system that could never quite dispel the twin aromas
of automotive enamel and charred mystery meat in a slurry
of convenience gravy. Worse, my kitchen was in the center
of the sprawling plant, and I had to walk past hundreds of
the raucous and frequently drunk production workers on
my way to it. "What are you burnin' today, Cookie?" or "Hey!
That Salisbury steak yesterday was SHIT!" greeted me every
day. I was soon looking for a way out.

That exit presented itself in a blind want ad that, alpha-
betically, followed the COOKS category in the Sunday paper.
Some anonymous firm was advertising for a COPYWRITER, and
since I had no idea what a COPYWRITER was, I had no idea that
I was unqualified for the position. I wrote a letter to that effect, also saying that it might be fun to get together and fill
me in on the definition of COPYWRITER, and sent it off to the
post office box listed in the ad. I then promptly forgot about
the whole thing. Six weeks later I got a call from the firm that
had placed the ad. I interviewed and was hired. During the
interview they told me what a COPYWRITER was, partly.

My career as a copywriter can be quickly passed over. After a single day on the job, I realized that I had been hired because *anybody* could get hired at this particular marketing communications firm. Talent or experience were really not parts of the hiring criteria. After I giddily gave my two weeks' notice at the Ford plant, I spent every spare moment teaching myself to type on an old Smith Corona. I had not picked up that particular skill in high school because the Christian Brothers had assured us that in our halcyon futures all such tasks would be performed by our secretaries. I remain a rotten typist to this day.

But such deficiencies were easily overlooked in the constant turnover of personnel. What we were selling was marketing communications, which meant everything from slide shows to movies to lavish company-meeting programs with all sorts of state-of-the-art electronic bells and whistles. In 1978, state-of-the-art mostly meant coordinating slide projectors with primitive computers and shooting lots and lots of billable 35 mm photos and 16 mm film. The art in all this was convincing our corporate clients that our work looked good and avoiding polysyllabic words in the copy.

The proprietor of this endeavor was a vesuviating alcoholic wife beater who imagined that his character defects somehow amounted to genius. That his clients saw it that way too may be a sad commentary on either the state of their perceptions or the state of the local competition for their marketing communications dollars. Regardless, he was highly regarded in some quarters, despite his wretched personality and ineptitude.

My own ineptitude was more than a match for his, but for a while I was successful, as far as his company was concerned. My screenwriting credits include the riveting *Thermo King Pit Stop Dealer of the Year 1978*, filmed in living color in picturesque South Boston. I also traveled to Forest City, Iowa, for inspiration for the lyrics to *The Winnebago Way*, recorded and performed at the motor home company's annual gathering of plaid-trousered sales varmints:

> When the road's a golden highway,
> Stretching westward toward the sun,
> And I want to do things my way,
> Not be rushed by anyone,
>
> I can climb behind the wheel,
> Any month or week or day,
> And the freedom that I feel,
> That's the Winnebago Wa-ay.

The next oil crisis all but put them out of business, but they did have a nice tune to hum in the meantime. And my boss made lots of money.

Alas, a year of this constant circus was about my limit. After a particularly gruesome day, I packed my cheap briefcase and walked out. I'm pretty certain that nobody missed me.

The one inadvertent benefit of my career as a copywriter came when I joined the company's sound engineer in a radio venture. A new community radio station with a whopping *ten watts* of power had just gone on the air in South Minneapolis.

He had joined up as a volunteer programmer and brought me aboard as his early morning sidekick. After a couple of months, the engineer got tired of doing the show and turned it over to me. I stayed on for four more years, broadcasting all kinds of music during ungodly overnight hours, when I could be reasonably certain that nobody was actually listening.

That was where I found myself in the late 1970s, with a string of unsuccessful jobs and nonpaying volunteer work in the depths of Jimmy Carter's malaise, to the tune of styrene disco music while wearing polyester pants. I'm sure I wondered if anybody else was actually having fun.

Crime Doesn't Pay (Unless It's Play)

We need to imagine that, at about the same time as I was bungling my debut as a short-order cook at the Ambassador, another young man was beginning his studies at the University of Wisconsin–Stout. David Berst's home had been in Milwaukee where he and his brother were raised by very strict, very Catholic parents. During high school, David had dreamed of working in the hotel business, mostly because it seemed to be a good way to escape Milwaukee and his family. He studied hard and got good grades but surprised everyone when the only scholarship he applied for was in hospitality management at Stout, which he easily won. He moved to Menominee, lived in a dorm, and learned that he, like nearly all the other students at that institution, whatever their respective majors, minored in alcohol consumption. He excelled in both endeavors.

David's appearance was that of an all-American boy, soft spoken and well mannered. He had bright blues eyes and a sincere look that encouraged trust from all he met. The manager at one of the college town's bars was so taken with David that, after hiring him to bartend, he discerned the young man's potential and offered him the closing manager's position after only a month on the job. David had not even finished his degree, and he already had his first job in hospitality management, a sinecure that offered him many advantages. For the rest of his academic career, neither he nor any of his friends ever again paid for a drink. What's more, he was able to pay his tuition in cash with banknotes that smelled strongly of beer and Jägermeister.

David was a thief, a lifelong compulsive pilferer. Throughout his career, he lived simply, never took a vacation, and came across as an honest, hardworking citizen, albeit a bit of a loner. He read voraciously, worked out with a personal trainer, and was loyal, often extravagantly so, to his few friends. This outward respectability served as a smokescreen that shielded David from all suspicion, but he was careful never to stay too long at any one job. Partly, he believed the longer he stayed with an employer, the greater the chance someone might put two and two together and implicate him in something. The other, more consuming reason was that, after he had pulled any particular con too long, he grew bored and needed a change of scenery and chicanery. David relished the joy of the chase, the thrill of the hunt. He was always on the lookout for his next quarry.

We first met in the early '80s when I was substitute teaching at a vo-tech college and David was the campus's food service manager. He was in charge of cash operations, food purchasing, and supervision of the student interns in his cafeteria. For whatever reason we hit it off well, and when my contract ran out and I left the college, David promised to keep in touch. He did so for over twenty years. Though we seldom saw each other in person, David often called me to talk, and gradually it became apparent that he *needed* to talk. The subject was almost always the latest bit of larceny he had perpetrated on an unsuspecting public. He described each scam in loving detail, and at first I thought he was just calling to brag about his exploits. As time went by, I realized that David was using me as his confessor. Although he stated that he'd like to have his exploits written down someday, it now seems evident that he wanted to unburden himself of guilt and receive absolution. From me! As a fellow recovering Catholic, I fell into this role more readily than I expected. Besides, David's revelations were always astounding and more entertaining than any caper fiction. He even provided sound effects during these conversations—the periodic tinkling of ice cubes in his glass.

Phone Call No. 1 (1982)

This conversation took place several months after I left the technical college where David and I met.

Phone rings. Picked up on the third ring.
STEVE LERACH: Hello.
DAVID BERST: Lerach, it's Berst. How are you?

SL: Fine. You?

DB: Much better, actually great. I finally quit the college.

SL: You quit? Why?

DB: Well, quit might be a little inaccurate. Actually my supervisor, Joe, and I came to a mutual agreement that I should never set foot in the place again *[laughs]*. If I do, they have the right to shoot me on sight.

Ice tinkling in DB's glass.

SL: Wow. What happened?

DB: Just a misunderstanding, really. Somebody needed to have a door unlocked or something, so for the first time in his bureaucratic life, Joe showed up earlier than his assigned 8:00 start time. He sees my pickup truck pulled up at the loading dock. That kind of brought things to a head.

SL: What was it doing there?

DB: Loading *[laughs]*. I don't think I mentioned my side business to you.

SL: No . . .

DB: Well, I'm the proprietor of a little company called Pinebrook Fine Foods. We do the meals for four fraternities at the University of Minnesota.

SL: Really? Can you make any money feeding frat houses?

DB: You can if you have almost no cost of goods.

SL: I don't get it.

DB: For the last year and a half, your tax dollars have been put to good use, nourishing students at our state's premier institution of higher education. Minnesota, Hail to Thee!

SL: You don't mean . . .

DB: Yeah. Every morning the Kraft trucks drop us a load of

groceries around 6:00, and at 6:30 my guy Bruce pulls up with my truck and helps me break down the delivery box by box. One for the college and one for Pinebrook. One for the college and two for Pinebrook, et cetera.

SL: Nobody notices?

DB: Nah, not so far. Look, all I had to do was coordinate the menu at the frat houses with our lunch menus here at the college and then order extra food. Bruce shows up and picks up the extra, goes to one of the frat houses, cooks it up there, and then distributes it to the other frats. I bill the frats SIX DOLLARS a meal *[laughs deliriously],* and my only expense is paying Bruce to do the cooking and keep his mouth shut. The student workers here at the college ruin so much stuff on a *good* day that nobody ever questions the amounts I purchase. And if one of the houses wants to have a special event with fancy stuff, I just find out what the culinary program here at the college is working with and up the order. America is a wonderful country.

Ice tinkling, swallow.

SL: But you got caught.

DB: Not for that. Apparently, there's been some problems with the cafeteria cashier's drawer not balancing. Actually, she's screwed up on a couple of occasions and taken too much.

SL: Margaret's stealing too?

DB: Well, not for herself. She's a Pinebrook employee, too. Look, six months ago there's a knock on my apartment door, and there stands Margaret, with a big welt under her eye. It turns out her husband, Nigel, this English prick, slapped

Margaret when he was drunk, and she ran out of the house. I felt so bad for her. She's scared and crying, a real mess.

SL: What did you do?

DB: What any concerned and caring boss would do. I invited her in, made her a drink, listened to her story, made her another drink, and then fucked her brains out. And hired her as a Pinebrook employee, in our Cash Recovery Department.

SL: So you had both wholesale and retail covered. Why are you telling me this?

DB: I'm not sure. I guess I need to tell somebody, and I thought you'd appreciate the elegance of the whole thing. Anyway, the school year is almost over at the U, and I've already told the frats that Pinebrook can't service them next fall, so I need to find something new to do.

SL: Well, keep me posted.

DB: Sure thing. Bye.

Saloons, Restaurants, and Reformers

Restaurant dining in the United States has always had something of an identity crisis. Early on, the country was largely rural and agrarian, with the produce of the hinterlands being consumed closest to its source. Seldom did the majority of the rustic citizenry venture far from their own hearths, and when they did, various boardinghouses and country inns supplied their dinnertime needs. These meals consisted of set, limited menus concocted by the local hostelries. Since much of the early United States had the misfortune of being first settled by natives of the British Isles (no siesta!), it was unsurprising that English, Scottish, and Irish foodways were followed by the population, adapting the native produce to traditional practice.

British and Irish cookery had their roots in the country, as well. Traditionally, the English elite derived its wealth from land holdings in the shires. After parliament prevailed in the English Civil War, political power was concentrated in London, and with their only options disreputable taverns and public houses, gentlemen dined in their urban clubs. Because of their country origins, the British gentry preferred the traditional fare available in rural areas. Overly fancy dishes were regarded with suspicion as an affectation that betrayed an effete Frenchness. Simple, hearty dishes—the roast beef of Merrie Olde England—were the staples of the British diet, a preference that accompanied their colonizing forces around the world.

In the young United States, arrivals from other parts of Europe, like the Delmonico brothers, brought new food notions to the growing urban areas. Here, disciples of French haute cuisine like Charles Ranhofer made steady headway in shaping the tastes of the Anglo-Saxon elite, while middle-class Americans remained grounded in simpler, more traditional fare. Choice of dining venues became a visible differentiator of class and wealth in nineteenth-century America, mirroring the situation of the previous century in France. By the time of the Civil War and the concomitant high tide of the Industrial Revolution, all American cities had at least a few of the French-inspired fine-dining houses. There, gentlemen regally consumed the elaborate dishes that displayed the triumph of French cuisine. As early as Tocqueville's time, Americans were noted for their huge appetites, amply supplied by the bounty of newly Indian-free farmlands, rich fishing shoals, and cheap immigrant labor. Renowned trenchermen, epitomized by wide-girthed financier Diamond Jim Brady, now showed their status not only by the quantity but also by the quality of their repasts.

But largely, it was gentlemen only at America's urban restaurants. Female diners feared tainting their reputations by association with restaurant dining rooms, unless they were already celebrities or already notorious in some less public way. Alcohol was the crucial factor in this divide. French-style restaurants necessarily utilized and served the wines, liquors, and liqueurs that pervade the French menu, and polite society made little distinction between the various vendors of Demon Rum. From the 1840s onward, pietistic Protestant congregations began to campaign for temperance in the consumption of alcoholic beverages. After the Civil War the drive for temperance was superseded by growing demands for outright prohibition of the manufacture, sale, and consumption of alcohol. Middle-class Protestant women were in the forefront of the Women's Christian Temperance Union and other organizations that campaigned for a "Dry USA." Denied the vote, women flexed their political muscles in this movement, and booze became an issue in virtually every election campaign nationwide. Saloons were smashed by bands of teetotaling female vigilantes, and they saw little difference between establishments that served alcohol. Many conflated restaurants and saloons as dens of iniquity, where their husbands and sweethearts were likely to drink and even enjoy themselves if not kept under strict female supervision. To the Anti-Saloon League, cognac and rotgut were equally abhorrent.

For the dry crusaders and the white upper and middle classes in general, the latter half of the nineteenth century was a disquieting period. The demographics of the United States were changing alarmingly. Immigrants swarmed into the country, beginning with floods of hungry Irish during the potato famine of the 1840s. The Irish were followed by Germans, Italians, Jews, and other eastern and southern Europeans, who had alien cultures that featured alcohol consumption as part of their makeup. Contributing to the uneasiness of the Anglo-Saxon elite was the arrival of waves of Chinese and Japanese from the West, as well as the encroachment of Hispanics and freed blacks from the South.

Restaurants gave these new arrivals to America's cities a way to stake a claim in the country's wildly entrepreneurial economy, as well as a place to relax and celebrate with other transplants from the old country. To reduce labor costs and maximize profits, immigrants who owned and operated a restaurant often employed every family member, which meant that women were now a visible part of the workforce, cooking in delicatessens, rolling pasta in *trattorias,* or even serving schooners of pilsner in their husbands' *Bierstubes.* For Anglo-Saxon women of the better sort, already infected with the righteousness of prohibitionism, the thought of their husbands being served by buxom *fräuleins* in some beer garden was anathema.

Their resolve grew. Their only consolation was that domestic servants had never been cheaper or more plentiful.

Phone Call No. 32 (Autumn 1991)

This conversation took place after David had been a sales rep for Kraft Foods, a large food-service purveyor, for about a year, where he acted as the liaison between the company and several large corporate clients.

Phone rings. Picked up on the second ring.
DB: Lerach? Berst. Sorry I haven't called lately.
SL: That's OK. I'm sure you've been busy . . .
DB: Really, really busy all summer. But I have been getting a lot of fresh air.
SL: You? You've never been much of an outdoorsman.
DB: Well, I've spent every Saturday and Sunday outdoors all day, all summer.
SL: Where at?
DB: At my homegrown-produce stand, of course.
SL: Oh no . . . where's this?
Ice tinkling in David's glass.
DB: *[Laughs.]* Out in Minnetonka, of course. Right on the side of a county road. Nice and shady. And I guess it really wasn't a stand, just a couple of banquet tables loaded with produce from my *farm*.
SL: Your farm?
DB: Well, actually from the Kraft warehouse.

SL: You just walked out of the warehouse with cases of fruits and vegetables?

DB: Of course not. That would be *stealing! [Laughs.]* You see one of my accounts is SkyChefs, the guys who do all the food for the airlines. They're big, and they buy hundreds of cases of stuff from Kraft every day. But the guy who does their purchasing is an idiot, so he's constantly calling me for will-call orders to cover stuff he's forgotten. So whenever he calls, I write up two invoices for SkyChefs—one for what he needs and one for what *I* need. I take both invoices to the warehouse, and they load up my truck and deliver to SkyChefs and, incidentally, to that warehouse space with the cooler that I'm renting. Since the idiot calls me every day for an order, by the end of the week, I've got a lot of stuff ready for my homegrown-produce stand. I smear a little mud on the melons and take everything out of the boxes that have a place of origin printed on them *[laughs]*. Did I tell you that I wear bib overalls and a straw hat at the stand?

SL: Business is good?

DB: Sometimes I have to go back to Kraft on Saturday afternoon just to get more stock. It's entrepreneurialism in action. People really like those locally produced fruits and vegetables, and believe me, the quality is excellent because I hand select every item. And my prices are really *reasonable.* Too bad the police showed up.

SL: Uh-oh.

DB: Oh, it's not a big deal really. I guess some of the local grocery stores are pissed because I'm taking away a lot of their business, so they asked the city council to check whether I've got a license to have a roadside stand. They send out a couple of cops. Now these cops have been some of my best customers all summer, lots of free stuff for them too. And when they find out I don't have a license, they *apologize* to me with all kinds of bullshit about how it's just not right that the little guy is always getting squeezed by the big stores, and they're very sorry, but I'll have to close down the stand . . . in two weeks! *[Laughs maniacally and long.]*

SL: But doesn't SkyChefs reconcile their invoices to their monthly statement? Why haven't they noticed that they're being billed for merchandise they didn't receive?

DB: Oh, that was the hardest part. They were refusing to pay for some of the deliveries they had no record of. So, a couple weeks ago I was up all night with some old invoices and an X-acto knife. I'd cut a line out real carefully, say for three cases of cucumbers, and then paste it onto a blank invoice. I did a bunch of these, hundreds of cut-and-pastes, with my delivery dates on them, Xeroxed them, and then brought them over to show them what they owed. They're so sloppy they just figured they had lost the invoices, and they paid up—in full!

SL: Wow, this is unbelievable! But it sounds like an awful lot of work for whatever little bit of money you could make selling vegetables. Was it worth it?

DB: Well, first of all, it was FUN. Besides that, last week I put down a big down payment on five wooded acres facing Lake Superior near Bayfield. That's for my retirement. It's truly the American Dream *[laughs]*. Gotta go. Bye.

* * *

Preference, Pretense, and Prohibition

By the 1880s, the United States had reached a form we would recognize today. The frontier had vanished, replaced by industrialization and urbanization, and the population was steadily climbing, in numbers and aspiration. The American middle class had seen unprecedented growth since the Civil War as new industries brought the need for an expanded managerial and technical class, both in the conglomerate corporations and in small businesses. Despite periodic recessions, depressions, panics, swindles, and scandals, more money was in the hands of the middle class than ever before. At the same time, new methods of shipping, preserving, and delivering foodstuffs made an array of products more accessible and less expensive than in previous years, and the cost of food actually fell steadily in the last quarter of the nineteenth century. The continuing overall prosperity of the middle class made it seem that everyone could be a Carnegie or a Vanderbilt, if not in reality then at least for some moments at the dinner table.

Though the specter of mass immigration may have been disquieting for the American elite, the resultant abundance of impoverished women needing work was a useful factor in middle-class pretension. Compared with today, domestic service in upscale and middle-class neighborhoods was ubiquitous. Maintaining a proper staff was the mark of a family's progress toward the American dream. Servant head count alone was important, but the ability of a husband and wife to entertain their peers elegantly was an even surer sign of success. Moreover, the wives of these unions, rather than being mere adjuncts of their husband's good fortune, could express their own worth by managing a successful domestic establishment, marshaling all their forces in gourmandizing display. Shut out of the voting booth, the saloon, and the restaurant, middle-class women could at least act as the major-domos of their own homes.

The servants themselves ran the gamut of newcomers pouring into America. In the Northeast, Irish and Italian girls were preferred, while in the South blacks maintained their traditional roles as the working underclass. Latinas came to the households of the West and Southwest, with a sprinkling of Asians along the Pacific seaboard. Domestic service offered them a step out of the teeming urban ghettoes, whether by day or by live-in service, in ampler households. Faced with the need for employment and the available options of stifling sweatshops or unhealthy textile mills, many women sought out what was available as maids, nannies, and cooks. The pay was low and working conditions varied with every domicile, but like all unskilled immigrants throughout U.S. history, they worked where they could and contributed their salaries to their own families' upkeep.

Of those hired to be domestic cooks, few had anything but the sketchiest training. Though some developed formidable skills on the job, most merely did their best to provide for their employers' modest mealtime needs. In an era before convenience foods, gas cookers, or even piped-in water, meeting these needs meant long hours of drudgery for the unskilled immigrant girls. The middle class of the time was still overwhelmingly Anglo-Saxon, and the execrable tradition of British cooking remained the predominant preference of polite society. Though a real, French-trained chef might be borrowed from a local restaurant for special occasions, for day-to-day meal preparation the domestic cooks turned out reliably overcooked, underseasoned, starchy, and salty dishes for their patrons. The nutritional experts of the day warned that spicy concoctions were detrimental to gastric good health, besides being the province of the hoards of social inferiors trooping in to Ellis Island. For the genteel, bland and predictable were the hallmarks of the daily menu and further confirmation of their elite status.

It should also be noted that consumption of alcoholic beverages in the home bore far less stigma than imbibing in a saloon or restaurant. In the home, decorum could be maintained by the mistress of the house, while men, left to their own devices at a public house, were far more likely to overindulge in everything overindulgible. Though many women maintained their belief in a dry America, most of their prohibition efforts remained in the realm of public alcohol vending. One of the symbols of domestic power was the possession of the key to the family liquor cabinet, and a prominent aspiration was that booze would appear nowhere else.

Phone Call No. 47 (1993)

When he made this call, David had left Kraft in order to set up another business. He called it Valley Distributing, and it consisted of himself, a refrigerated straight truck, and some rented cooler space in a warehouse. Using the customer contacts he made while working at Kraft, David was then selling fruits and vegetables to a small, but growing, clientele.

Phone rings.
SL: Hello? Oh David, I had a feeling you were going to call.
DB: Why . . . have you heard something?
SL: No, no. It's just been a while.
DB: Pretty busy these days, now that I'm CEO of Valley Distributing.
SL: CEO and everything else on the table of organization, I'm assuming.
DB: Well, yeah. Believe me, I don't need any disgruntled employees shooting off their mouths. Besides, a lot of people don't enjoy working only in the dead of night *[laughs]*. Plus it's hard to get a truck through an alley with the headlights shut off.
The usual ice in the usual tumbler.
SL: How's business?
DB: Right now it's a Republican's wet dream! Did I tell you I picked up the contract for all the produce for the whole local chain of Baja Tortilla Grills? I made a nice presentation to the district manager six months ago. They liked my product and my prices—they had been using Kraft before—so they decided to take a chance on Valley.
SL: How big a chance are they taking?
DB: Huge! Fourteen stores, and they use a lot of lettuce, tomatoes, and avocadoes. They're busy too. Lunches are huge,

and dinner is growing fast. That's why they need a supplier with my *flexibility*.

SL: Nothing more flexible than a snake.

DB: I resemble that remark *[laughs]*. Listen to this—*they* actually tried to shake *me* down. Twice!

SL: I bet that cost them some money.

DB: Ohhh yes. After I've been delivering to them for a month, their district manager calls me in and asks if I can sharpen the pencil a bit. You know, cut my prices. So I shoot him an offer: Yes, I can knock about seventy-five cents off every case if I can do "after hours delivery." I feed him the line that delivering to all those locations of his in daytime traffic eats up my time and raises my costs. But if I show up at 4:00 AM everything is quicker and easier.

SL: They have staff in these places at 4:00 AM?

DB: No, but he wants the price break, so get this: HE GIVES ME THE KEYS TO ALL HIS STORES!!! *[Maniacal laughter.]*

SL: What an idiot.

DB: Yeah, but that's not the half of it. He runs all these places with two managers: daytimes and nights. College kids who don't give a fuck. Since I'm so flexible, it means that I let the night managers call in their orders for the next morning before they close the store. They have to guess how much product the morning crew will go through, and since they don't want to take any shit from the morning guys about outages, they always order high.

So let's say the guy orders four cases of tomatoes. I get there at 4:00 AM, and there's three cases already on the shelf in their cooler. I deliver one additional case and bill them for four. Sometimes when I get there, there's actually five cases already in the cooler. Then I *take* the extra case, leaving them with four, invoice them for four cases, and deliver the extra one to the next store. Some weeks I sell the same case of tomatoes to as many as three of their stores. And I do this with everything they buy from me. Since my sale price per case is still lower than Kraft's, they think they're actually saving money. I'm the P. T. Barnum of produce!

SL: Wow. How long do you think you can ride this particular pony?

DB: Practically forever. See, two weeks ago the Baja district manager calls me up and says he wants to have a little chat with me. I'm thinking, "Uh-oh, this bonehead has finally smelled a rat!" So I go visit him one afternoon, and there's no police cars in the parking lot . . .

SL: Good sign.

DB: The two of us have a little heart-to-heart talk, and he tells me how much he appreciates the good service and the reasonable prices, and he just *knows* I appreciate his business. And in order to show my appreciation, he wants me to kickback a hundred bucks a week to him personally, off the books, to cement our relationship.

SL: Of course, you were shocked.

DB: Absolutely! I practically bit through my lip trying to keep a straight face, but in the end I gave in. He has no idea how much that extra hundred bucks is going to cost him!

SL: W. C. Fields said, "You can't cheat an honest man."

DB: I wouldn't know. I've never met one.

SL: Back up a second. How did you ever manage to offer him

such low prices in the first place? After all, Kraft and the others have a lot more buying power than you.

DB: And a lot more overhead. They'd be even more expensive if they had decent security.

SL: What do you mean?

DB: Oh, I haven't told you how I spend my Saturday mornings.

SL: Ah, no.

DB: Well, before I quit Kraft, I managed to acquire one of their delivery driver jackets and hats. So, in full uniform, I pull my truck up to their dock every Saturday morning, when the weekend relief crew is working. I wave at all the guys—I must look vaguely familiar to them—and walk into the sales office. I've got all the computer codes, so I download all their customer accounts and price lists so that I know what they're charging everybody for everything. Believe me, this is useful information when you go out on sales calls, especially when I'm working their customer base.

SL: You have brass balls.

DB: Sometimes it's even better. A few weeks ago, I'm in there getting my lists, and as I'm leaving, I notice a whole pallet—sixty cases—of avocadoes just sitting there. And I look at all these avocadoes, and they're really expensive right now, but I remember that I had left my pallet jack at the warehouse, so I shrug my shoulders and start to go. Just then, some warehouse fuckhead cruises through on a forklift. So I asked him to give me a hand. He says, "Sure," and loads them into my truck. Five minutes later, I had to pull off to the side of Lone Oak Road because I was laughing so hard.

sL: Unbelievable.

DB: You know what's really unbelievable? That week, my total cost of goods was *negative* 15 percent! America the Beautiful. We'll talk soon. Bye.

Ice tinkling. Click.

As I hung up the phone, my wife asked me who had called. When I told her it was David confessing a new scam, she began a lawyerly cross-examination.

"Why hasn't anybody caught on to this guy? He's been pulling this stuff for years."

"I think it's because he's so bold that nobody can believe it. Also, he looks so straight and, well, normal that it's like he's above suspicion."

"Let's get one thing straight: *You* aren't getting involved with any of this, are you?"

"No. I'd screw up, get caught, and *you* would probably testify against me."

"So you condone what he's doing?"

"Not at all, but what am I gonna do? Call up some company and tell them they're getting screwed by their tomato supplier? Look, you probably won't understand, because you've never worked in restaurants, but there's all kinds of people in the industry who are just trying to preserve what they see as their freedom, their individuality. They couldn't work in cubicles or factories making widgets. Every day they struggle to express themselves, whether it's making a better batch of soup or getting a customer to run up the guest check or, in David's case, pulling a bit of larceny that nobody's done before. The impulse is the same—do it better than yesterday. Step back and tell yourself 'nice work.' They've learned that the only rewards that matter are the ones you give yourself."

"Still, don't get involved."

"How could I ? If I did anything but listen, I'd be violating the sanctity of the confessional. You can go to hell for shit like that."

Alley Sustainability

Increasingly, idealistic chefs are preaching the gospel of locally sourced, organic, sustainable ingredients. They enter
into partnerships with local farmers, swineherds, cheese
makers, vintners, wild-raspberry pickers, dandelion har-
vesters, and truffle-sniffing dogs, in a back-to-our-roots
campaign to bring traditional, renewable food resources to
concerned diners. These diners will drive their suvs any distance and pay any inflated menu price in order to feel that
they've somehow helped to save the earth. After all, free-
range chickens that are allowed to eat insects, as well as the
intestines of their less aggressive flock mates, just naturally
taste better, especially at twice the price.

Partnerships with local producers are nothing new, although those terms are. At my next major career stop, as
sous-chef and eventually executive chef at Schiek's Cafe, we
practiced felonious collusion with black market smugglers.
And the prices we paid were always *lower* than those offered
by the legitimate purveyors, who only paid lip service to the
free market. We encouraged true entrepreneurialism by giving all the little guys a shot at our business, as long as no actual shots were fired.

My first encounter with these submarket forces came
one springtime afternoon. There was a loud banging on the
restaurant's back door. On opening it up, I found two Native
American guys in sunglasses near an aged Oldsmobile with
the motor noisily running. They were standing out of the
sunlight, smoking cigarettes, and looking like there might

just be plenty of reasons for looking as suspicious as they did. One of them spoke to me while his partner nervously scanned the alley.

"Hey, Chef, you guys serve walleye?"

I was about to answer in the affirmative, but my attention was riveted on the old, old Oldsmobile. It was rusted up to the fenders and carried Red Lake Reservation license plates, American Indian Movement bumper stickers, and a dream catcher dangling from the inside mirror. There was nothing particularly unusual about that, here in precasino Minnesota, but the fact that a steady drip of water was puddling under the rear of the vehicle seemed a bit odd.

"Walleye?" I asked distractedly.

Well, of course we served walleye. At the time walleyed pike, *Stizostedion vitreum,* appeared on every menu in every restaurant in Minnesota. It was broiled and deep-fried, filleted, sautéed, and puréed. The pike's mushy blandness made it a favorite of diners with those same traits, and each serving augured up fond memories of overlong stays at mosquito-infested cabins up north. The stuff was iconic, overfished, and increasingly expensive, and most of the locals had no idea that the Minnesota walleye they were devouring came mainly from Lake Winnipeg in Manitoba.

While his partner kept watch, one of the Ojibwe brought me over to the rear of the dripping Olds and popped the trunk with a screwdriver. Inside, under a layer of rapidly melting ice cubes, was about two hundred pounds of random-sized walleye fillets. Some were from old lunkers that yielded sides as long as your forearm, while others were palm sized from fish that the Department of Natural Resources might have used as evidence in court. All were fresh, sweet, and priced right. I raided the petty cash drawer and bought the lot and even went to the bar to get them a couple of road sodas for the long return trip back to the reservation.

After that, the unpleasantness at Wounded Knee and all those inconvenient treaties were forgotten as these two accepted me as the Great White Chef who dispensed money and beer. In the fall I was able to purchase newly harvested, unpolished wild rice, with superb flavor and substantial savings, from the same trunk of the same Oldsmobile. At that time I was also promised a bumper crop of choice cuts of venison, especially that of the hard-to-find fawn variety (whitetail veal), but they did not return. Since we had never had any contact other than their random visits to the alley behind the restaurant, I had no idea what became of them.

Others proffered their goods in the same manner. There was a rough-looking bearded guy who tried to sell me corn-fed wild boar that tasted like conventional pork and a guy who ran jerry cans of maple syrup in from Wisconsin ("Sorry, we don't even serve breakfast here"). The best by far was, however, a pale, furtive little man who showed up once, and only once, each spring. He had the look of a college professor who ventured out into the sunlight once, and only once, per year, but that was quite enough. *His* trunk was filled to the brim with musty, lusciously fragrant morel mushrooms. A trunk full of morels is a breathtaking, expensive sight, but the mushroom man would answer no questions about their provenance or even give us his right name. He seemed haunted by the idea that someone might discover his secret woodland morel grotto, where, no doubt, a troop of fairies propagated and harvested this fungal treasure. He carried a very accurate scale, quickly weighing out the amount we specified, even breaking a morel in order to achieve the exact desired weight. Then he was off to the next alley behind the next restaurant to peddle his wares. Meanwhile, we were putting Walleye in Morel Sauce on the menu.

6

Fromage

Sous

There is no better job in restaurants than sous-chef. This second-in-command position makes everything happen in the kitchen. The sous directs the actual operation of the feeding machine, trains and teaches, and can generally be counted upon to keep order in the midst of the near chaos that is every service period in a busy operation. The sous has just enough authority and not too much responsibility. Though nearly everyone defers to the sous, he or she generally manages to avoid the ultimate responsibility of cost overages, human resource crises, and fretful ownership. Whereas executive chefs are the ultimate temporary employees, at-will retainers who are sometimes gone in an eye blink, sous-chefs, if competent, can ride out most storms by just keeping their heads down and getting the job done. At worst they may be a member of a departing executive chef's entourage, following the alpha chef to his next assignment. I really liked being a sous-chef.

After the copywriting debacle I naturally gravitated back to the milieu. Though I tried freelance writing for a time, my landlord didn't feel that I should defer rent payments until my paltry royalties arrived. The paltriness of the remunerations was richly deserved, as a glance through your collected back issues of *Interstate Truck Trader* will show. Luckily, most of the trucking plagiarism I cobbled together for this august journal went unread, as the majority of the publication consisted of lurid ads for backstreet massage parlors and escort services. I sent out bales of submissions to other, tonier publications and stopped saving rejection letters after I had a drawer full. I was forced to quit smoking just to save money, and without sweet nicotine as my muse, my literary career seemed doomed.

But you can always get a job in a restaurant, and since a friend from my Ambassador days was an executive chef at a suburban country club, I visited him and let him talk me into a part-time job making sandwiches for rich golfers. Not thirty days later, my friend's sous-chef showed up for work gloriously drunk and was loudly fired in the middle of the kitchen. Without missing a beat, the executive chef turned to me and asked whether I wanted the sous-chef job or not, godammit. I accepted.

There were a few old hands from the Ambassador there,

so most of the crew was familiar to me. My abrupt elevation opened a vacancy in the pantry, however, and at the height of the golf season this position had to be filled immediately. One of the other cooks brought in a candidate he had met at downtown Minneapolis's Gay 90's. He was a thin, boyish-looking man about my age named Michael.

A Few Words from Michael

Wel-l-l-l-l, I was wondering when I'd get back into this little story. Way too much hetero-sweatero garbage so far. A *girl* like me can't seem to get any consideration!

Most of what he's been saying is true . . . but bor-ing. Gawd. Anyway, yes, they hired me to make sandwiches and do display work and so forth out at the Minneapolis Golf Club, which isn't in Minneapolis at all but out on the end of the bus line in some stupid suburb. It took *forever* to get out there on the bus, but I did my crocheting or slept the whole way.

The kitchen crew was ok, but the general manager of the place was an old nelly in a three-piece suit with a Phi Beta Kappa key on his watch chain. A real queen. I might have even tricked with him once, but I must have been *really* drunk at the time. Anyway, whenever I got sick of those straight people in the kitchen, he'd let me do some serving in the dining room, which kept me from going absolutely insane. As a new guy and a fag as well, I took a lot of shit. I'd walk in on Monday, and some punk would yell, "Hey Mike! Ya get any pussy this weekend?" and I'd have to answer, "They were pussies, all right." Or some shit. The best was when this very straight bar manager—such an ass!—was trying to strike up a conversation with me while I was making his sandwich. He asked me if I had a nice day off yesterday. "Oh *yes!*" I gushed. "I met a couple of guys at the 90's, and we ended up getting into a lovely three-way." *He* never bothered me for a sandwich again.

Since the buses barely ran out there at night, I'd usually ask the sous-chef if he'd give me a ride downtown to the 90's after work. After all, he lived in South Minneapolis, and it was only five miles or so out of his way. He told people that he made me ride in the trunk. I think he was pretty amazed that I *never* went directly home after work. He didn't want to hear about what I was doing *every* night, unless I came in with my glasses broken or had a welt on my head. But as long as none of it affected my work, nobody cared.

Our sous-chef changed employers a few times in the early '80s, and I always went along with him. He must have thought *I* made him look more manly or something. He was kidding himself! So when he and the executive chef went on to run the kitchen in a restaurant by Lake Calhoun, I went along. When that place closed, he got the sous-chef job at Schiek's Café, and you know I followed him there. Hell, that place is only two blocks from the Gay 90's! I sometimes think he took that job just so he wouldn't have to give me any more rides.

* * *

Schiek's

Friedrich Schiek left Germany with an armload of recipes
and a dream of opening a high-class establishment. Reaching Minneapolis during the Civil War, he found that only a
few boardinghouses and ramshackle hotels served to feed
the population of what was then a frontier boomtown. He
worked in some of these establishments, slowly putting
away some seed money for his dream restaurant, and in 1887
Schiek made the dream a reality.

Schiek's Café was a dimly lit but highly ornate Victorian
confection. Schiek brought in wood-carvers from his native
Germany, as well as Italian tile and stained-glass artisans, to
embellish his restaurant. On a muddy street in downtown
Minneapolis, the café originally served hearty German fare,
fine wines, and schooners of local beer. The place immediately became the finest restaurant in the city, largely by de-
fault, and later maintained that status as its chefs broadened
the menu to include all sorts of European specialties. Schiek
enhanced the appeal of his restaurant by installing a separate
ladies' entrance, which conducted them through a circuitous
route, avoiding the smoky saloon portion of the premises,
directly to the dining room. Friedrich's sons carried on the
tradition after his passing, and though it relocated several
times and changed ownership periodically, Schiek's Café
maintained its reputation for exquisite cuisine in plush
surroundings for nearly a century. Before the onset of Prohibition, it set the standard for fine dining in Minneapolis
and elevated the general standard for restaurants locally as

its competitors strove to match Schiek's. Even today, the elegance reputedly continues, although recently in the guise of a gentlemen's club, Schiek's Palace Royale, and nekkid ladies have replaced food as the primary attraction on the menu.

The building that housed (and houses) the latest incarnation of Schiek's Café was originally a bank. It was built at the close of the nineteenth century, when bankers believed that an imposing edifice was their best advertisement for the bank's safety and stability. The walls were marble, and the floor was mosaic. Dark wood was everywhere, and crystal chandeliers hung from a curlicued dome that soared above the premises. The stateliness of the bank building alone could not guarantee, however, the safety of the depositors' funds. The old bank was connected to the rest of the Minneapolis downtown area by a labyrinth of tunnels, where couriers could do the bank's business out of the purview of desperadoes. During Minneapolis's growth spurt just before World War I, the bank outgrew its palatial space and relocated after selling the building to the Schiek family of restaurateurs. They converted the building into a plush, multichambered dining facility just in time for Prohibition and the Great Depression. The restaurant's fortunes rose and fell for the rest of century.

Ownership changed repeatedly after Prohibition, but they kept the Schiek's name. The café was revived under a series of proprietors, finally reaching its height of fame in the 1950s and 1960s. A local businessman named Ben Berger had bought the ailing café and invested enough money in the place to bring it up to the elite circle of Minneapolis restaurants.

Charlie's, Freddie's, Harry's, Murray's, and the Dyckman Hotel were the restaurant's main high-end competitors, but Schiek's alone could boast the musical stylings of the Schiek's Sextet, a string ensemble made up of moonlighting musicians from the Minneapolis Symphony Orchestra. The food was decent but grounded in middle-class cookery, as were all the other upscale restaurants of the time. By the 1970s the critical mass of customers in Minneapolis had migrated to the suburbs, and downtown restaurants began closing one by one. Berger sold off Schiek's and went off to tend his other enterprises, including some successful pornography outlets. The old bank building housed a series of failures through the 1970s, including a purveyor of red sauce wretchedness that billed itself as the Spaghetti Emporium, which miraculously managed to bankrupt itself serving pizza and pasta. A new consortium of owners purchased the building on the cheap shortly thereafter and decided to resurrect the only thing that had ever made sense at that location. Schiek's Café was reborn.

Nutritionists to the Rescue!

What I am calling "middle-class cookery" had its origins in the last decades of the nineteenth century, and in its own way, this style of cookery was revolutionary. Not only was it driven primarily by women, unlike the French haute cuisine of a hundred years before, but the newest scientific breakthroughs contributed to its popularization. And for the first time women were prominent among the contributing scientists.

The explosion of scientific discoveries in the Victorian era was nowhere more profound than in the medical sciences. The treatment of physical ailments was at last free of superstition and the archaic practices that had held sway for centuries. Instead, medical men earned a new credibility and prestige as empiricism replaced snake oil and effective treatment supplanted the bone saw. Medical practitioners even went beyond the symptoms of disease and sought to discover its causes. Since the ingesting of foodstuffs was the one universal practice among the ailing public, there was a sudden scientific impulse to discover whether food choices could be analyzed and scientifically associated with the choice between health and disease. The science of nutrition resulted, taking over, in the medical hierarchy, from the science of phrenology.

Largely denied access to medical schools, educated women with a scientific bent found their niche in the budding nutrition discipline. There was no lack of theories to pursue in this new science, and oftentimes the ideas tended to cancel each other out. Germ theory argued that foods should be cooked to a sanitary mushiness, whereas the discovery of vitamins argued against overly processed preparations. Disciples of Horace Fletcher (who were actually called "Fletcherists") postulated that every mouthful of food required a minimum of one hundred chews in order to be beneficial to the body. Bleached white flour was seen as the closest thing to a perfect food. Some, like the Kellogg brothers, even equated dietary purity with spiritual perfection. Nutrition science has never really shed its evangelical underpinnings.

The lady nutritionists also found themselves becoming social workers. Finding malnourishment in the immigrant ghettoes of American cities, they attributed dietary deficiencies to the gastronomic preferences that the newcomers had brought with them from the Old World. Spices were obviously aphrodisiacal, accounting for the higher birthrates among immigrants. Fresh fruits and vegetables from the pushcarts that plied the teeming streets carried germs of unknown and dreaded provenance, and nutritionists promoted commercially processed and preserved foods as the antidote. Huge, heavy breakfasts, instead of bread or bagels, would help immigrant children in the public schools. Eating white foods— rice, potatoes, chicken, and veal—would settle their fiery foreign temperaments. The new powdered baby formulas would lower infant mortality, brought on by suckling at the polluted breasts of non-Anglo-Saxon mothers. But there was one ingestion problem that the lady nutritionists could not allay unaided: Irish whiskey, German beer, and Italian wine still stood as obstacles to nutritional perfection on earth.

Nutrition science formed the intellectual underpinnings of middle-class cookery. The "servant problem" of the early years of the twentieth century made this cookery de rigueur in most middle-class homes. Immigration quotas were drastically lowered in those years, while job prospects for lower-class women broadened considerably. Sweatshops had been unionized and cleaned up. Typist and switchboard operator jobs were becoming available. Even factory work, especially during World War I, was no longer off limits to women who needed employment. These positions, though often menial in their own ways, still offered reasonable pay and regular hours, unlike those of domestic servants, who were always at the beck and call of their parsimonious employers. The supply of those seeking domestic-service jobs dropped drastically, and as Adam Smith might have predicted, the cost of the remaining domestics rose so that only the truly wealthy could afford them.

For middle-class women this meant a return to the kitchen. Husbands and families still made tremendous demands for regular meals and social occasions, but now the wives of the managing class had to largely go it alone. In some towns and cities, congregate dining schemes, actually involving the cooperative purchase and staffing of dining houses, were attempted, but they failed to catch on. In other places caterers were employed but were too expensive for everyday service. Moreover, after years of reliance on hired help, genteel American women could not be expected to take that step down the social ladder.

American business and industry came to the rescue. Spurred on by the new nutritionists, commercial food companies flooded the market with new food products. They championed the scientific purity of their products to a public still horrified by muckraking books like Sinclair's *The Jungle*. Innovations in shipping, preservation, and packaging meant that even corner stores could carry the latest offerings. These products were designed for convenience and the strictures that food scientists were popularizing. More important, for the first time national manufacturers, with their advertising power, began to dominate the market. The labor-saving benefits of various brands could now be conveyed directly to the harried housewife, as could the nutritional wonders that could be performed. Since they were national brands, they had to appeal, of course, to the broadest spectrum of potential consumers, so midrange flavor profiles were ideal and ease of use was essential. These products undoubtedly were a godsend to the homemakers of the time. Since, in most cases, gastronomic expectations had never been raised by semiskilled hired cooks, there was not much room for disappointment when their places were taken by well-meaning wives. A bowl of cornflakes was quicker, easier, and supposedly about as nutritious as bacon and eggs. Powdered whipped-potato mix beat the hell out of peeling actual potatoes. Canned vegetables were always on the table in five minutes. Gas stoves and other new cooking technologies made meal preparation quicker and less laborious. Within two decades middle-class cookery, with its roots in the British Isles and its scientific pedigree fully branded, was the national gastronomic vernacular. Only in the increasingly assimilated ethnic communities and in French-inspired restaurants did cooks exceed popular expectations. Alas, their time was running out.

Vending Vernacular Victuals

My arrival at Schiek's in 1981 was propelled, almost literally, by the demise of my previous employer. As sous-chef at the Top of the List, a restaurant on the uppermost floor of a high-rise apartment building overlooking Lake Calhoun, I had an elevated opinion of my progress and prospects. This establishment and the apartment building, along with lots of other pricey real estate, was owned by a local fat cat who had married into a fortune and was determined to enjoy it all. And so he maintained the skyscraper dining room as the jewel of his real estate and hotel empire, where he could impress his guests with an Icarus-like view of Minneapolis, with his many and varied holdings studding the landscape. Like most restaurants with a view, the vista outside the windows was considered sufficient to bring in the dining public.

In truth, the food on the menu followed the general course of middle-class cookery to which I had become accustomed since the beginning of my restaurant career. In the Minnesota heartland, over a thousand miles inland and insulated by forest and prairie, the food served to local diners was much as it had been since the Jazz Age. Meat and potatoes alternated with fowl and potatoes, with the occasional fish and potatoes thrown in during Lent. A typical night out consisted of several rounds of cocktails, followed by a relish tray of oxidized carrot and celery sticks and an inevitable iceberg lettuce salad, often studded with artificial bacon bits the color of old scabs. Then the pièce de résistance would thud onto the table, perhaps an eighteen-ounce serving of prime rib or a porterhouse the size of a newborn. Each creation was accompanied by a foil-wrapped baked potato (gold foil in nicer restaurants) and a tub of sour cream, which might alternately be incorporated into last night's baked spud as the notorious twice-baked potato. Frozen vegetables could be had à la carte. This feast could be washed down with a tumbler of Mateus or Lancer Rosé, no vintage, just off the tramp steamer from sunny Portugal. Then followed baked Alaska or perhaps a flaming cherries jubilee, prepared tableside by a maître d' who could reliably, and often, vouch for the quality of the *Kirschwasser.* Finally, a few more drinks or some no-name coffee would propel the diners out of the restaurant and onto the freeway, occasionally in the right direction.

The meal described above could be had at any decent restaurant in any city or town across the United States at any time after the imposition of Prohibition (minus the booze). For those of us who worked in kitchens, the learning curve for producing such meals was a short one. The ingredients we worked with were straightforward and universally available, and the skill level required for their preparation, beyond basic butchery, mostly involved timing and endurance. In a very real sense, the mastery of supper club cooking was akin to the crash course that middle-class women went through when their domestic servants evaporated. The quality of the product met most expectations, even those of the owner of the restaurant atop the high-rise building.

What the owner of the Top of the List wasn't expecting was, however, the onset of a fatal case of small-cell cancer of the lung. When told to get his affairs in order, closing a money-losing restaurant appeared near the top of his list, right after "get chemotherapy." The employees reached street level jobless, and each went his or her own way to find something new. The very next morning, after a valedictory siege of a nearby bar, I boarded a bus downtown to visit the unemployment office. Also aboard the bus was an acquaintance from some crew in some restaurant in some time past. He too was looking for work, in a desultory way, and had heard a rumor that Schiek's Cafe was looking for—wait for it—a sous-chef!

The Dry Desert

A crushing blow for fine-dining restaurants in the United States was the passage of the Volstead Act on October 28, 1919. The Eighteenth Amendment was ratified soon after, and the nation launched into the Noble Experiment—Prohibition. A remarkable political consensus approved proscribing the production and sale of alcohol. Northern Republicans and southern Democrats joined the Prohibition Party and Progressives in general in abolishing the vice of imbibing spirits. Certainly, various religions championed the cause as well, notably the Methodists, Baptists, Presbyterians, and other pietistic sects, but Prohibition stands as one of the culminations of the Progressive Era, along with woman suffrage. Though northern capitalists and southern hellfire preachers were Prohibition's most vocal champions, American women, especially middle- and upper-class women, were its primary beneficiaries.

Fine dining at the time was universally French or at least French inspired. Such cuisine required the use of wines and liqueurs for both its creation and enjoyment. Moreover, the restaurants that offered this expensive, demanding, and labor-intensive menu needed the extra income that the sale of alcoholic beverages brought in order to make ends meet. This consideration meant little, however, to Protestant middle-class women, also some of the most fervent advocates of Prohibition. For them the abolition of alcohol service in restaurants meant that they could enter those establishments without being tainted by scandal. Restaurant dining would no longer be the preserve of men, and one more bastion of male exclusivity would cease to exist. Just as important, a trip to a restaurant could be a couple's locus of socializing and entertainment, liberating the wives from their kitchen duties.

The problem was that the restaurants themselves were struggling for survival. Even if they managed to maintain their former haute cuisine in a bastardized dry configuration, demand for that style had virtually evaporated with the alcohol supply. As women and families became a bigger portion of the restaurant clientele, they showed their preference for the style of cooking—middle-class cookery—to which they had become accustomed. A general revulsion with all things European after the Great War contributed to the desire for simple, plain, and familiar dishes, the kind of things that had sustained Americans since their arrival on these shores. Restaurants that could adjust to this shift by dumbing down their menus had a chance to survive. Those that did not simply closed, and their staffs moved on to tearooms, department store cafeterias, and other more egalitarian dining houses that sprang up to fill the void. Tragically, saloons were transformed into soda parlors. The irony is that, while the numbers of the dining public grew, the variety of dining experiences on offer shrank considerably. The ethnic restaurant segment did expand and become more popular, but these places were largely looked down upon by genteel Anglo-Saxons. Their preferences remained in the realm of middle-class cookery, a prejudice that would long survive Prohibition, the Great Depression, World War II, and my own entry into the world of restaurant practitioners.

A Belated Renaissance

With all the other sous-chef jobs on my résumé, it was pretty easy to land the position at Schiek's Café. By then I had a feel for managing small groups of barely professional cooks turning out unspectacular food for an undiscriminating public. None of my expectations matched, however, the reality on the ground at Schiek's. First of all, the executive chef and most of the crew consisted of young, eager cooks, some of whom had actually attended culinary school. Even those without formal training nurtured a passion for good food and a willingness to innovate in creating dishes that went beyond middle-class cookery. The first stirrings of a revolution in the culinary arts had finally made it to the Midwest, and new restaurants with new ideas were opening up all over town. Apparently, as usual, I hadn't been paying attention.

The revival of all things food related as a source of passion had been going on for a few years. In the previous decade *nouvelle cuisine* had swept France and advanced across the Atlantic. Its practitioners, with a nod to nutrition science, had concluded that the older forms of traditional cooking, with rich sauces, fussy preparations, and multiple courses of massive portions, were hopelessly passé. Instead, French chefs began advocating leaner, more natural preparations for which they could charge even higher prices to their credulous clientele. Two blocks away from Schiek's, the New French Café opened as the main local purveyor of the nouvelle.

The American media had already prepared the public for a change in the old order. From the mid-1960s onward, Julia Child was appearing all over public television with her *French Chef* program. Julia's (she was always "Julia") *Mastering the Art of French Cooking* was a best seller. Almost single-handedly she had demystified fine cooking and opened her viewers and readers to the possibility of dining creatively and well as the natural order of things. And cheaper, faster air travel meant that more and more Americans vacationed where this had always been true. Carrying things even further, another innovator, Alice Waters, opened her restaurant Chez Panisse in Berkeley in 1971. Waters emphasized the preparation of locally produced, mostly organic foods. Her inspiration too was French, but Chez Panisse pioneered what came to be known as California cuisine, a cooking style that rapidly spread inland from the West Coast.

As if things weren't complicated enough, a new wave of immigration was taking place in the wake of a decade of warfare in Southeast Asia. Suddenly, lemongrass and *nam pla* (fish sauce) were becoming commonplace ingredients,

joining relatively recent arrivals like salsa and falafel on restaurant menus. As always, the new immigrants started their
own ethnic eateries, but their influence was felt throughout
the industry.

The 1980s were a turning point for American restaurants. By this decade most families had both parents
employed outside the home, leaving little time for meal
preparation. Increasing affluence and interest in dining
possibilities brought back the restaurant as a social focal
point, a phenomenon unseen since two centuries before in
Paris. Throughout the United States there was an explosion
of restaurant openings. Chain restaurants went beyond their
fast-food origins and evolved as dinner houses. Ethnic restaurants flourished, transforming whole neighborhoods into
dining nodes, accessible by car from everywhere. Independent restaurants, often driven by chef-owners, proliferated,
offering the public more choices and more faddish places to
be seen at, served at, and bragged about. Traditional middle-
class cookery, though far from extinct, became just one more
option on an expanded menu of possibilities for the diner.

I had stumbled right into the middle of a revolution, and
I didn't even know it. Now what?

Michael's Turn

Ah, you'd better let Michael answer that before you get your
undies in a bunch—ooh, not a pretty picture at all. Anyway,
when I heard that my old sous-chef at *two* other places was

now at this hotshot Schiek's Café, I started bugging him for a job. After all, a *girl* has to make ends meet. He finally talked the chef there into hiring me to make desserts when the pastry chef flamed out.

It was a pretty normal setup: Most of the cooks were straight; *all* the waiters were gay; and there were just a few fag hag waitresses for color. A bunch of the cooks were artists or musicians or students, and there were plenty of crazies all over the place. During lunch and dinner, we served all the business people and lawyers, and at night, after dinner, the place turned into a disco, full of hairdressers and Iranian guys wearing way too much cologne.

Bringing a fag into the kitchen violated some taboo or some shit—gay guys were supposed to be waiters—so early on I took more crap than usual and gave plenty back in return. I remember one night when this big bouncer—he was really built—walked through the kitchen, and one of the cooks yelled, "Hey Mike, how do you like that one?" So I answered, "If I stick my dick in his ass, he'll probably just FLEX and snip it off!" which had most of the cooks laughing. All except one redneck kind of cook who turned, got angry, and yelled, "Michael, if you don't knock off that fucking faggot talk, I'm going to take you out in the alley and kick your ass!" So I *squealed,* "Oooh, my kind of MAN!"

After that I got along great with everybody, at least until the exec chef left and the sous-chef got promoted to the top job.

The Happy Hour War of 1984

Though there are no monuments, veterans' associations, or commemorative medals, few participants will ever forget the Happy Hour War of 1984. Survivors are still reticent to discuss the horrors experienced or the scars still suppurating on their souls. For those who have attempted to put these painful events out of memory, I apologize for reopening the wounds here.

The primary battleground of the Happy Hour War was downtown Minneapolis, and the root causes of the struggle could be found in the darkest recesses of every entrepreneur's psyche. A brief upturn in the economy after the first Reagan recession increased business at downtown bars and restaurants, sometimes dramatically. The proprietors of the establishments who survived the previous year or two of middling business found their cash registers tinkling again. Their Pavlovian reaction was not satiety but the irrepressible urge to cash in even further. They sensed there was money loose on the streets, and they were going to get their share.

As competitors, however, the restaurateurs realized that raising prices to increase revenue meant that savvy customers would shop around until they found a bargain. That was out. Resorting to trade journals and hospitality organizations, the owners discovered that people were in the habit of eating three meals per day most days. Though they could slip a brunch in here or there, it was unlikely that the dining public could be persuaded to expand its daily meal schedule to include a fourth or a fifth meal. Two-for-one coupons, take-out options, and media promotions proliferated, and they brought in customers, but most failed to increase profits because they offered discounts on the food only, the item that cost them the most. Merely increasing discounted food sales was no ticket to profit.

The real money was in liquor sales. The real problem was convincing people to drink more, but that's never been much of a problem. Late afternoon liquor sales had been rising, and nearly every booze vendor was doing whatever they could to continue the trend. In this, they were aided materially by the chronic undercapacity of the Minneapolis metropolitan area's freeway system. Rather than wait out the rush hour traffic that was stationary on the area's third-world road net, downtown office workers headed for a watering hole to pursue an alcohol agenda until the roads cleared. Happy hour drink specials, two-for-ones, and even three-for-ones proliferated downtown, and cubicle dwellers were nightly rubbing lubricious legs with their coworkers.

The Minneapolis city fathers, horrified that anyone might actually be having a good time, sensibly began counting up the carnage engendered by those lingering too late at happy hour before embarking on a decidedly unhappy journey homeward. Threats and imprecations were showered on the bar owners for sending hordes of bleary-eyed Dodgem car drivers onto the freeways. Police patrols were beefed up. The specter of the breathalyzer hung over the celebrants. The saloon proprietors began to sense a cave-in at the gold mine.

In a desperate effort to slow the rate of alcohol absorption while maintaining the afternoon drinking craze, most bars and restaurants considered adding food to the mix. Chefs all over downtown were ordered to create new appetizer menus for their bar trade. Tiny hamburgers proliferated. Deep-fryers were clogged with molten mozzarella sticks. Ersatz dim sums came steaming out of kitchens. Spies were dispatched to neighboring restaurants to see what the competition was producing and how much they were charging the patrons. The rivalries heated up. All appetizers were reduced in price; then the price was cut in half, fixed at one dollar—free with a limited-time coupon! The cutthroat competition mushroomed like stuffed mushrooms, and when prices for the bar food could go no lower, the frenzied proprietors decided to do away with pricing altogether. The food would be given away for free, and dammit, THEY WOULD COME.

War is hell, or at least heck, especially when a chef is trying to maintain a reasonable food-cost budget. When the decree came down that every weeknight twelve feet of banquet table space in the bar was to be filled with free goodies for the drinkers, it seemed likely that I would spend myself out of a job. But the owner of Schiek's could not be made to see reason. Still, a brief argument convinced him to allot a pretty generous food budget to be written off as a worthwhile expenditure in his bid for victory in the Happy Hour War. Free money means fun.

The kitchen staff, augmented for the purpose, was soon having a wonderful time producing all sorts of unusual delicacies. We ground up carloads of pork butts for exotic sausages. We bought cheese from Ireland, butter from Normandy, and most of the 1984 squid catch for *ceviche* and fried calamari. Kalamata olives? Not exotic enough. A keg of Mount Athos might be more interesting. How about smoked sea scallops? Baby octopus in olive oil? Can we make *our own* mozzarella sticks with hand-pulled cheese and *panko* bread crumbs? Sure. Why not? We've got the budget.

This madness continued for a couple of months as all the nearby outlets put out their free hors d'oeuvre buffets and hoped for the best. Happy hour business would increase in one place just as word of a better spread elsewhere would draw the customers away to another. What's more, the war was having a decidedly deleterious effect in another part of our business. Instead of sticking around and buying a real dinner, a great many of the happy hour crowd merely loaded up on free finger food and then went bloatedly reeling off onto the streets, leaving our dining room empty. Most of us realized that we were playing a zero-sum game.

Not the owner. He was determined that ONE FINAL SURGE would bring him victory in the Happy Hour War, and he would go forward in spite of cost, casualties, or credibility. He reasoned that most of his happy hour customers were single, young, urban professionals ("yuppies," as they were just beginning to be known), so what better way to secure their allegiance than by hosting the MOTHER OF ALL HAPPY HOURS? Besides offering a nightly two hours of cheap food and drink, he would institute a monthly singles' night and do his happy hour thing into the wee hours. There would be drinking, dancing, and a couple hundred eligible singles mingling around the Schiek's cash registers. He would play cupid and Toots Schor to all the beautiful people in Minneapolis. After singles' night every other bar owner would be forced to acknowledge his triumph.

Meet that Special Someone
Singles Night at Schiek's!
Free Hors d'oeuvres

When the big night arrived, our skeleton kitchen staff prepared trays of appetizers for the two hundred upscale customers we were expecting. We got four times that number. Not only had we underestimated the turnout, but it turns out we had even more grossly overestimated the "upscale" part of our projections. The place was jam-packed with desperate, ravenous, inebriated, terminally horny revelers. The halfway houses and trailer parks were emptied that night as every lonely gnome who could scrape up bus fare descended on the hapless restaurant. Losers and leaches, hookers and harelips, widows and wetbrains gyrated in the airless bar and dining room. Wedding rings slipped into pockets, and newfound lovers slipped into stairwells to seek clumsy consummation. The bar was so crowded the patrons couldn't head-butt their way into it, and the cocktail waitresses left in despair when they could not penetrate the penetration-minded throng.

The hors d'oeuvre buffet, the nicest we had ever prepared, was instantaneously stripped by the lecherous locusts. They were soon whooping and shouting for more food, and the wild-eyed owner ran into the kitchen seeking something, anything, to put on the table and quiet the outcry. The reduced kitchen staff began pulling anything edible (and cheap) out of the coolers and freezers, heaping things onto trays and into ovens and generally fighting a losing rearguard action against insurmountable odds. Michael was fuming as he slapped together new cheese and vegetable trays under intense pressure. "By the time I get all this shit finished, there'll be nothing left but fat guys at the Gay 90's!" he wailed. Since the service station was set up on the opposite side of the building, any runner attempting to bring food replenishment from the kitchen had to thread his way through a seething sea of hunger and concupiscence in order to accomplish his mission. I forced my way though on several occasions, shouting, "HOT STUFF! COMING THROUGH!" in the din, to no avail. On one of my last missions, as the supplies were running out, I had my only satisfaction of the evening. As I attempted to bully my way through the crowd, a balding, puka-shell-wearing hipster tried to reach over my shoulder to grab a chicken wing from the pan I was carrying. Bringing my right elbow up sharply, I caught this slime sharply under the chin hard enough to jangle his yellow teeth and then kept moving as he lisped curses after me. After that, we just ran out of food.

For the owner, singles' night was a chastening experience. Not only had he seen very little revenue for his troubles, but he had to preside over closing time and the spectacle of the most loathsome remaining singles finally hooking up. There had been no yuppies and little money, and his restaurant had been trashed by the milling mob. The next day he raised the white flag. No more singles' nights, not even any more happy hour giveaways. Humiliated, he would return to operational sanity. We in the kitchen savored the defeat.

7

Dessert

Executive Chef

One of the first things I saw when I walked into the kitchen at Schiek's Café was a cook with a whole raw salmon on his head. Actually, it wasn't a whole salmon; it had been gutted, and the cook had placed his head into the slit in the belly and was duck-walking behind the high pick-up counter in the front of the kitchen. There before me was a huge, dead fish swimming along in midair, with the cook concealed behind the stainless-steel counter. The other cooks, the dishwashers, and the waitrons were all laughing uncontrollably. (We actually called the servers "waitrons" there. Referencing the ethnicity of some of its nighttime patrons, the garbage dumpster in the alley was known [unforgivably] as the Cherokee Buffet. It was that kind of place.)

The busier the restaurant, the greater the need for stress relief, and Schiek's was busy. That relief took many forms. A couple of the staff were stand-up comedians when they weren't slinging hash. There were also painters, actors, a dancer or two (with or without brass pole), some students, and the usual complement of drinkers, dopers, and deviants. But on the job they were professional restaurant staff of the highest order, who accomplished prodigies of valor, serving a demanding public and having fun in the process.

My favorite was Wayne, the maintenance guy. He was a beer-bellied man in his thirties who had worked in the place for over ten years. The old building had seen so many different repairs and remodelings over the years, by about five ownership groups, that Wayne was the only person on earth who knew where every valve, switch, and hiding place was located. Each successive owner of the building came to realize that they could not operate without Wayne, the Living Blueprint. So for the most part Wayne played the gnome, sitting in the labyrinthine basement of the building among the ducts and pipes and boilers, smoking dope and waiting for the call when the next piece of critical equipment should fail. Part of Wayne's sinecure was his assignment to be first on duty every morning to clean up the disco area from the previous evening's revelries. Most mornings he was able to find enough misplaced street drugs and paraphernalia to make his lonely daylong vigil more tolerable.

As in most restaurants, the rest of the crew was something of a movable feast. Turnover was brisk as other establishments or professions or the witness protection program siphoned off Schiek's employees. Eighteen months after I arrived as sous-chef, the executive chef that I reported to was lured away by a better job in a better place. The easiest thing for the management to do was to offer me the job, minimizing disruption and saving considerable salary outlay. In 1982, I accepted the executive chef position. My starting salary was $19,000 per annum, no fringe benefits.

What the owner of Schiek's got for his $19,000 is open to dispute. Certainly, he got a lot of time on the job—seventy to eighty hours a week—plus competent supervision of lunch, dinner, parties, and catering. And effective purchasing. Pretty good security. Even loyalty. But the bottom line is that, in my own terms, I wasn't much of a chef, title and princely salary aside.

First of all, there was the food. As a major player in a reviving downtown restaurant scene, Schiek's was supposed to be a culinary destination. My predecessor had been, and still is, a genius with food. He was a natural cook with excellent instincts for flavor and a knack for innovative dishes and presentations. Though I had had decent on-the-job training and far more experience, most of my work had been in middle-class cookery, and for a chef, I actually found cooking rather boring. My solution for covering my own deficiencies was to hire the finest cooks I could attract, buy them the finest ingredients, and take the credit for their work. I managed this charade for two and a half years, successfully most of the time.

My other major defect was in not adopting the stereotypical persona of the Chef. The idea that the head chef in any kitchen should be a back-of-the-house autocrat was a deeply held tradition. Ranting and killing with looks, hiring and firing at will, and maintaining a kind of steam table sovereignty were all the prerogatives of the chef, and I had worked for several who had played this role like a Barrymore. Though this petty dictatorship certainly had its appeal, I deemed it too much work for a fairly limited reward. The one thing that working for chefs like these had taught me was that I never wanted to be like them, and though I could strike the pose on occasion, I always felt naked and not a little ridiculous. Therefore, since I had already hired better cooks than I could ever hope to be, I tried whenever possible to run a collaborative, somewhat democratic operation, at least among the cooking staff. This seemed like my own Noble Experiment. Instead, this peculiar regime regularly turned chaotic as various participants jockeyed for position, shirked real effort, or pursued their own twisted visions of how a kitchen should operate in an authority void. As things turned out, I spent more time managing the process of managing the kitchen than I did managing the kitchen. Another charade.

There was only one area where I had to assert absolute authority—the dish room.

Notable Dishwashers

The china plate placed before the customer, with its accompanying silverware and glassware, is undoubtedly more valuable than the foodstuffs riding upon it. The chemicals used in washing and sanitizing that plate are often more costly, ounce for ounce, than any soup or sauce the cooks can concoct. The machine that performs the washing process is always the single most complicated and expensive appliance in a restaurant kitchen. Naturally then, the persons operating this vast dishwashing system are the least motivated and the most poorly trained and pitifully compensated members of the restaurant staff. How could it be otherwise?

Proportionality is seldom a strong suit in restaurant management. The idea that a $250,000 machine, with crucial connections to water, drains, electrical, steam, and ventilation systems, should be placed in the hands of minimum-wage, semiliterate, frequently stoned employees is breathtakingly perverse. Further, expecting those employees to flawlessly handle thousands of dollars' worth of expensive smallwares and table settings and a bewildering variety of beverage glasses several times each shift—under extreme time, temperature, and temperament conditions—is the triumph of hope over experience. Nevertheless, such is the situation in most professional kitchens.

This discontinuity plays itself out in a number of ways. On the positive side, the dishwasher with a modicum of reliability and competence is treasured like a rare pearl and protected, pampered, and provisioned in a manner that exceeds the expectations of that lowly status. But even the astute ones are seldom promoted until they can be effectively replaced. Replacing a good one is always difficult, sometimes impossible. This lag often leads to the dishwasher's discouragement and subsequent departure, leaving only some soiled aprons and drug paraphernalia behind. Cleaning out a terminated dishwasher's locker can be a macabre adventure.

And recruitment of dishwashers can be a dicey process. Perhaps the greatest possible mistake is to put a help-wanted ad in an urban newspaper and require qualified applicants to show up at such-and-such a time, at such-and-such a place. I actually did this once at Schiek's. The resultant gathering resembled the barroom scene in *Star Wars,* as desperadoes from every fringe of the galaxy stumbled in, not only at the allotted time but hours and even days before and after. Dozens of the old and grizzled lined up with the young and frazzled, and clearly the plasma center across town had a slow day. All got an application form, but some, it seems, were just after a free ballpoint and departed, leaving the form untouched. Others had to request a second or third copy as they forgot which name they happened to be going by that week. Still others merely stared at the paper with no comprehension of what the printed black marks on the page could possibly represent. Though I interviewed some thirty-five applicants one day, none of them could remotely be considered for actual employment. And I was desperate.

This marathon was occasioned by the imminent departure of the Hobart Brothers from Schiek's for their annual migration to the Soil. The Hobarts weren't named Hobart, but they did operate a dish machine with a nameplate with the ubiquitous brand name "Hobart" emblazoned upon it. These two were sixties leftover hippie-hillbillies who moved to the country in the summertime to raise and smoke organic produce. Though they promised to return in the fall, the odds were slim that they would actually remember to do so. If they did return, they brought much of the Soil back with them in their hair and beards and in the secret places of their bodies. Occasionally, on their return, another such child of god would accompany them, lured by low wages and the opportunity to wear sandals even in the dead of winter. Though the Hobarts were absent for at least three months of the year, they were still more reliable than their replacements.

John was one such replacement. When interviewed, he seemed alert and intelligent—always a bad sign. Still I hired him, and he worked hard, was cooperative and uncomplaining, and seemed ecstatic to be a dishwasher. The cooks would see him working at this station across the kitchen, talking and laughing, scurrying with plates or pans when they were requested and generally behaving in a highly suspicious manner.

One day as I walked toward him at the scrape table, I noticed he was talking away, with nobody else around him.

"John, who the hell are you talking to?"

"Oh hi, Chef. I guess it's kinda obvious who I'm talking to."

"Really? Well, fill me in here. Who are you talking to?"

"The dish machine."

"And *why* are you talking to the machine? Are you lonely or . . . something?"

"Not any more."

"Oh."

"Besides, she started talking to me, and it wouldn't be very polite if I didn't hold up my end of the conversation, would it?"

"It's a 'she'?"

"Well, yeah. Anybody can see that."

"Sure . . . right . . . Ah, what do you guys talk about?"

"Oh all kinds of things. How busy it is. How her rinse temperature is running. How my day is going. All kinds of things. She encourages me, tells me to do a good job."

"Hmm. Well, you two are doing a great job, John. Carry on."

Naturally, I didn't dare repeat the details of this conversation to anyone. I reasoned that a roaring case of schizophrenia hardly disqualified John from his chosen vocation, but knowledge of his condition might make the rest of the crew slightly nervous. Besides, any discussion of John's situation might be overheard by the dish machine and repeated to John during one of their tête-à-têtes. One more eccentricity would hardly be noticed.

Every relationship has its rough patches. A couple of weeks later, John came to my office and, with a heavy heart, announced that he was putting in his resignation. I was shocked; he and Miss Hobart had seemed so happy together. John explained that the dish machine was no longer confining her communication with John to his work shift. John said that she was now talking to him day and night, wherever he happened to be. What's more, she had turned hostile, trying to boss him around and demanding more and more of his time. He felt his only recourse was to quit his job, leave town, and break all his ties with the dish machine. His mind was made up.

I tried to reason with John. If she was talking to him outside of work, what was to prevent her from doing the same thing, albeit long distance, after he left town? Had he given her an ultimatum, demanding that she behave herself or he would cut off her chemical rinse agent and force the shame of streaky glassware upon her? Was there no hope of reconciliation? Was there something I could say to her to get her to back off?

Who was really crazy here? Good dishwashers are hard to find.

John's successor was an older, mostly toothless gentleman by the name of Meyer. He wore a greasy baseball cap and wraparound sunglasses at all times because, he explained, his retinas had been damaged during some service in some war, which was about as specific as Meyer got about anything. He proved to be a competent worker for a time, in spite of his occasional rants about how nobody among the other members of the crew would ever truly understand the extraordinary Meyer.

One extremely busy night, the dish machine suddenly stopped, and Meyer was nowhere to be seen. Searching furiously for him, I found him lying behind the dish machine, either dead or just temporarily comatose. I was about to shout his name when I noticed that, for the first time in memory, Meyer was not wearing his foul cap. Furthermore, the cap was lying beside his prostrate old body, and the cap itself was neatly lined with aluminum foil.

I shook him, and he immediately lunged for the cap and jammed it back on his head. I asked what was going on. "Thank God ya found me when ya did, Chef," he replied. "They done it again! I was just wipin' some sweat when I took this here hat off. If this hat is off, then BANG! the *Gimps* put a ray on my ass that puts me right to sleep. Shit, I think you musta saved my life!" But I couldn't save his job for long, and within a week or two, the Gimps apparently triumphed and Meyer stopped showing up for work. But then Fidel Castro came to my rescue.

One of the bearded dictator's most charming habits was his periodic emptying of all the prisons and insane asylums in Cuba and sending of their former inmates to the United States. In the spirit of Reagan-era anti-Communism, we accepted all these hapless *cubanos* yearning to breathe free, gave them a new homeland, and gradually incarcerated them one by one as they reverted to form. Local social service agencies assisted in this process, and one of them, the local Catholic Charities, made me an offer I couldn't refuse.

That agency's allotment of Cuban men needed employment, and I, as ever, needed dishwashers. The social worker and I quickly struck a deal, and the next day Jorge and Victor were delivered to the back door of the restaurant. Jorge was a stocky brown little guy, apparently middle-aged, with an appealing, jocular manner and the ability to work hard. He had gotten on Fidel's bad side because of his propensity to put on women's clothing and sashay around, cooing in a Spanish dialect that was amazingly both falsetto and a bit guttural. There was no guarantee which gender Jorge would affect on any given day, and the cooks were soon wagering beers over it regularly. Sometimes Jorge showed up in men's clothing but painted up with rouge and mascara. Those days each cook bought his own drinks.

Jorge's compatriot was a taller, younger black man named Victor. We weren't told why Victor had spent time in a Havana jail, but he had obviously spent plenty of it. His eyes were menacing yellow slits that accommodated inky pupils with which Victor constantly scanned his surroundings, on the lookout for trouble. His hair resembled an explosion in a mattress factory, and on his cheeks and arms he carried old, cruel scars that told of recklessness and resilience. He worked hard but showed a temper now and then that served to ward off casual acquaintance. Victor's knowledge of English was on the sketchy side, unlike Jorge, who unaccountably knew a lot of nautical and sexual jargon. People joked with Jorge, but nobody joked with Victor.

One morning I got a call from the police station. It seemed that one of my employees had been arrested the previous evening, and the cops were looking to be rid of him if only they could find someone to make bail and take custody of him. His name was Victor. The policeman on the phone assured me that Victor had done no violence or committed any felonies that day, so could I please, please come and get him because he was raving in some Spanish dialect that not even the Mexican custodians down at the jailhouse could comprehend and demanding that his "Jhef" be summoned to deliver him from this ignominy.

In exchange for giving the bailiff fifty bucks, I received a form detailing the charges being leveled against Victor. Victor had been arrested for driving a twenty-year-old station wagon the wrong way down a one-way street . . . downtown . . . with no license plates . . . and no windshield . . . and no

passenger side door . . . while making out with his girlfriend
. . . playing salsa music at full volume from an enormous
boombox . . . steering with his bare feet . . . and having no
driver's license, identification, insurance, or the brains that
God gave turtles. They set a court date and made me promise to remind him to show up. I told the bailiff I would, but
he and I both knew it would never happen. Victor and I returned to the restaurant.

Victor resumed his position, with its daily ups and
downs, and managed to keep things together for a few weeks.
On a busy Saturday night he vanished, leaving the dish machine running and scads of dirty plates stacking up. The primary difference between chefs and cooks is that cooks don't
wash dishes. Spewing profanity, I took over the dishwasher
position for a couple of hours until unaccountably Victor returned. It was obvious that he was just passing through.

"Victor! Where the hell have you been?"

"Jhef, I gotta go!"

"Whaddya mean you gotta go?"

"Jhef, I go home to . . . to get something, and I find Jorge
and my girl! They fuckee mucho! I pull out my knife and stab
Jorge one . . . two . . . three times in the belly!"

"Jhef, I gotta go!"

"Victor, you gotta go."

Though it was not the only time that I had lost two dishwashers in a single night, it was probably the most singular.
I finished washing dishes, mopped the area, and went home,
knowing I'd have to call Catholic Charities on Monday morning to check on the availability of Cubans. I wanted to call the

police, but I had no idea where the alleged stabbing had taken place or in which direction Victor had made his getaway.

When I arrived at work on Monday, a message from Catholic Charities was waiting for me. Jorge would be out of work for a week, and in his place they were sending a couple of brand new Cubans. I shouldn't expect Victor any time soon (fine!). Sorry for the inconvenience. And Jorge did return a few days later, very sore and not as cheerful. He told us that the police had done a perfunctory investigation of the incident, but since Jorge wasn't pressing charges and since they were both just Cubans, the cops had just let it drop. Also, Jhef, could Victor get his job back?

No.

Retreat and Advance

On the night of December 23, 1984, I bought a final beer for all the cooks at Schiek's, wished them a Merry Christmas, and left the building at my usual 11:00 PM quitting time. I was beat. I had worked double shifts every day, including Sundays, since Thanksgiving to handle the glut of holiday business. All had gone well, and I felt tired but satisfied. Now I had a full three days off for the holiday, and it seemed as if I had just been paroled.

When I left the restaurant, snow was drifting down in giant flakes, and the whole world was a Currier & Ives print. Zooming home on the slushy streets, I walked into the house and demanded that my wife put on her coat and boots and

join me with a bottle of Jameson Irish Whiskey. The three
of us went over to Minnehaha Falls, a few blocks from our
house in South Minneapolis. The falls are in a park at the
heart of the city where the sizable Minnehaha Creek takes a
sixty-foot plunge before emptying into the nearby Mississippi. In the belly of winter, the falling water forms a giant
ice grotto, and people come to ooh and ahh at the spectacle at
all hours. The snow was still slowly falling in flakes the size
of commemorative stamps as we toasted my parole with a
shot of Jameson, wished each other Merry Christmas with a
second, and then trudged home warm and happy.

Naturally, a pregnancy ensued.

More than anything, the sudden expansion of our family
hastened the end of my career as the chef of a stand-alone
restaurant. Clearly, I was about to have responsibilities that
transcended those of kitchen boss, especially one tied up
with a massive time commitment, irregular schedule, and
puny salary. Besides, my wife had a career she had no wish
to abandon in favor of permanent childcare, especially when
her spouse, having worked extensively with mousses and pâtés, was far better suited for dealing with the contents of dia-
pers. She agreed to handle the breast-feeding herself, but I
would have to seek a more regular job.

That job came through a blind newspaper ad seeking
a chef for catering duties, a task I generally enjoyed. As it
turned out, the employer was a food service company, Marriott, which held the contract for feeding the patients and
staff of Mt. Sinai Hospital in South Minneapolis. Mt. Sinai
had been built by Jewish doctors in the early (*post*-Holocaust)

1950s when the other local hospitals refused to let them practice in their institutions. Now, in the 1980s, faced with competing with other megahospitals in town, Mt. Sinai was seeking to set itself up as a boutique sort of operation with luxury amenities, including superior victuals. They came up with the unique idea that employing a chef might be a good way to improve the food. I was the first chef to head a hospital kitchen in the Midwest, and a kosher kitchen at that.

When Mt. Sinai finally foundered, Marriott sent me to head the kitchen at another, much larger hospital. Once again, regular hours, higher pay and benefits, and the ability to mostly write my own job description kept me in place for another five years. I found that it's generally best to be the first one in your job classification. Nobody but you really knows what you're supposed to be doing. Moreover, with a more regular schedule I could attend T-ball games and birthday parties and offer my son much needed instruction in bat swinging, bike riding, and the intricacies of manly toilet usage. I had a good thing going.

Thus, it was with some trepidation that I took David's suggestion and applied for the brand-new campus executive chef position at the University of Minnesota in 1993. After more than a century of running its own creaky food service operation, the university had decided to try one more spasm of reorganization before giving up on the idea of feeding itself altogether. The university's food service was in disarray, morale was low, and the food product well and truly sucked. Nevertheless, I thought it might be an interesting—and lucrative—opportunity, and after a lengthy interview process,

I was hired to oversee all twelve kitchens and eighteen service outlets on the campus. They apparently didn't regard a 2.56 GPA as a barrier to my employment. I went in and remodeled restaurants, rewrote menus, and uptrained as many cooks as I could. But the university's food service was hemorrhaging money faster than we could sell pizza. It was fun while it lasted, but eventually the administration decided to cut its losses and contract the whole mess out. This time I went to work for the Aramark corporation, briefly. It was my final chef's job.

Employment by food contractors brought me into a setting that looked much the same but differed substantially from my experience working in restaurants. All the stainless-steel equipment, tiled floors, and humming ventilation fans failed to camouflage the fact that the nature of the work was changing rapidly. The most noticeable difference was the personalities inhabiting institutional kitchens. These were, for the most part, long-term professional employees in relatively strong unions. Many had attended vocational schools for culinary training and lived in stable family situations. There was nothing spectacular about the food they produced, but the customers were satisfied with the tried and true, so the cooks were quieter, steadier, and more conventional. They were a stark contrast to the colorful pirate crews to which I had grown accustomed.

In institutional food service we operated on the middle track of what was evolving into the three-tier model of dining seen almost everywhere today. On the very bottom are ubiquitous fast-food outlets, holding a greasy hegemony over a clientele that values speed, predictability, and low prices over relaxation, challenge, and quality. The second tier, by far the largest, is that filled with ethnic restaurants and, in an odd juxtaposition, the remaining purveyors of traditional middle-class cookery. In this bracket we have also witnessed the amalgamation of immigrant cuisines and the plain fare that has been the mainstream of dining for three centuries in America (think Chili's and P. F. Chang's). Salsas have supplanted catsup to some extent, and the dining public shells out a bit more money than at the quick-service counter.

The top tier of restaurant dining today is definitely once more in the hands of chefs, whether on their own as proprietors or in chef-driven corporate venues. Over the past thirty years various burgeoning influences have created a revolution in restaurant culture that echoes events in Paris two centuries ago. The dining experience has become increasingly free of the strictures that have existed here since Prohibition as chefs have sought to transcend the boundaries that separated traditional haute cuisine (thank you, Julia Child) from the multifarious ethnic cuisines that followed migration into this country. Another striking addition to the mix has been the drive to recapture the purity of ingredients and to source them from local producers (thank you, Alice Waters), all in the creation of menu dishes for a savvy clientele (thank you, Food Network). The go-getting chefs brought up in this world have for the most part received their training in the thriving culinary school segment and then gone on to seek work with other acknowledged masters before striking out on their own. This was pretty fast company, and I wanted no part of it.

My so-called career had always been a series of happy coincidences and fortuitous accidents. My training, while solid in the day-to-day performance of duty, was nowhere touched by the visionary or passionate mind-set that a real chef needs for success today. Though I surely appreciate the relentless drive for perfection that characterizes the best of chefs, I never felt the need to sacrifice all it would take to achieve that end. Rather, I was satisfied with knowing I may have helped some others on this journey. And if I have not helped them all, at least I have been witness to their efforts. My feet still hurt just as badly, but now I can rest them in a dining room chair on the other side of the swinging kitchen door. But when I dine out, I find myself peering into the kitchen, never without envying those folks in their white jackets. They are younger, browner, and more gender-balanced, and they have taken the place of those of us who have gone before—and those of us who are just gone.

Phone Call No. 81 (2004)

This conversation occurred after a couple more career changes for David. Because his little fly-by-night produce company was so profitable, it attracted the attention of one of the large local fruit and vegetable wholesalers. That company bought out David for a substantial sum and made him a partner and vice president as part of the bargain.

Though this position was lucrative, it was also numbingly boring for David. He couldn't very well steal from himself, and the new employer proved to be relentlessly honest. Though he tried to go straight for a year or so, things just didn't work out, and he quit. During the interim he had also gotten married and divorced, leading to a loss of a Minneapolis home, his Bayfield property, and lots of money. In an effort to lower his visibility for a while, he took a job driving for a messenger service, which brought him to the vulnerable back doors of many businesses. Before he could capitalize on any new opportunities, however, David was involved in a serious traffic accident, injuring his back, legs, and neck.

Phone rings
DB: It's me, Berst. Hi.
SL: Hi! I've been trying to call you. How are you feeling?
DB: Better, but still shitty. You?
SL: Fine. Last time we talked you were still having fainting spells.
DB: Yeah, that hasn't changed. If I stand up for too long, I faint, and if I sit for a while, I get nauseated and throw up. It's a great fucking life.
The usual ice in the usual glass.
SL: I can hear that you're taking your medication as we speak.
DB: *[Laughs.]* Yeah, there's a nice "pharmacy" right near my apartment. They deliver too. One-quart minimum.
SL: So what are you actually *doing* these days?
DB: Well, I'm helping out a buddy of mine doing work in his

catering kitchen. Before that I was feeling sorry for myself, but I realized what a trap that was, so I got over it. Do you know that I haven't done anything illegal or even dishonest for *over a year!* It's a disgrace.

SL: Don't tell me you found Jesus.

DB: Not at all, although when I was in the hospital, I did get a visit from the Buddhist chaplain. I guess I must have filled out the admission papers wrong *[laughs, coughs]*. No, I haven't been converted. I'm not even unhappy, even when I hurt bad.

SL: How often is that?

DB: All the time. Look, the way I see it, I can't complain. I've owned and ran three different companies, and I've lost more money than most people will ever make. I've pulled off so much shit, and I've never been prosecuted . . . or shot. Hell, it's been FUN! I've had a good run.

The only thing that really bothers me is that you're about the only one who knows most of the story, and believe me, I haven't told you everything. It would make a pretty good novel, but I doubt if anybody would believe it. Maybe you should write it some day.

SL: Maybe I will. I'll sit down with you sometime over some beers and just let the tape recorder run. Of course, we'll have to wait on publishing it until the statute of limitations runs out.

DB: Oh, it's running out. It's running out every day. Gotta go. Bye.

Click, slowly followed by another click on my end.

In November 2004, I got another phone call. This one was from David's employer, whom I knew vaguely from occasional David-related social events. He called to tell me that, when David had not shown up for work that morning or answered any of several phone calls, he had gone over to his apartment. He expected to find him drunk. Instead, he found him dead. The autopsy stated that David had gone into a diabetic coma after hitting his head on the porcelain in his bathroom. He was forty-seven.

Logan's Bowl of Soup

Shortly after I took the reins at Schiek's, I had a particularly distinguished customer in the dining room. It was a busy Saturday night, and my contribution to the menu on Saturdays was a pot of soup du jour. Making soup in restaurants means cleaning out the cooler for ingredients, and this night the pickings were sparse. I finally spotted a derelict roast leg of lamb, a few vegetables, and some cream—the makings for scotch broth. This was a concoction that Chef Logan had taught me years before. All the ingredients go into a food processor and get ground up together. Thence to the stove top for a touch of heat and a little seasoning, followed by some cream to finish the dish. All told, about fifteen minutes prep time— my kind of cooking. I made the scotch broth not knowing that Chef Logan himself would be our guest that evening.

When the waiter told me that one of his customers wanted to say hello, I walked into the dining room and found John Logan already on his fourth beer. Since he always ordered two at a time, I knew he really hadn't been there all that long. We talked briefly, and he let me know that he was moving to Seattle soon for a new job. I could talk to him for only a moment as the evening's customers were pouring in, and he understood completely. We promised that we would get together before he left town, both knowing that it was unlikely to happen. It didn't. It was the last time I ever saw Chef Logan. He died in 1996 at the age of fifty-nine.

Back in the kitchen, Logan's waiter told me that he had ordered two more beers and a bowl of scotch broth. I dished the soup up myself and sent it out. Awhile later, the waiter came back in and told me that Logan seemed to have liked his soup. How could he tell? At his first spoonful he had smiled and exclaimed, "The Son of a B-B-Bitch learned what I taught him!"

Michael Demands Yet Another Hearing

Blah-blah-blah. We're certainly not getting back to Michael very regularly, are we? Always a bridesmaid, I guess. Anyway, Schiek's was mostly a cool experience for me. The chef only fired me twice. That's right, twice. But that was in two and a half years, and since he had fired me everyplace else at least once, he really wasn't up to speed with me at Schiek's. The worst time was when I asked the bartender if I could use the phone at the 90's. So I called in the afternoon and told the chef I was *(cough, cough)* really sick that night and wouldn't be in that night. He says "ok," and the next thing I know he's walking into the bar and practically dragging me off the barstool and making me come to work. Such a bully! Didn't even let me finish my cocktail.

Anyway, the chef finds out his wife is pregnant, and all of a sudden, working eighty hours a week doesn't seem like such a good idea to him. *I* could have told him that! Everybody knew he was looking for a different job, even before the baby was born. Oh, that was funny. On the day his wife called from home because she was going into labor, the chef comes running out of the office, putting his coat on, and shouting, "The water broke! The water broke!" Wayne the maintenance guy was standing in the kitchen at the time, stoned out of his mind. He yells, "Oh shit!" and grabs his pipe wrench and runs down to the basement looking for a flood.

The chef goes to work for a big food service company running the kitchen at Mt. Sinai Hospital. You know, regular hours and a dental plan, or some shit. It takes him a couple of months, but then, as usual, he hires me to work for him making kosher Jell-O and low-sodium egg salad. But this place was about to go belly up. Too small and too ghetto. So the company decides to transfer the chef over to United Hospital in St. Paul in September of 1987, and before he leaves, he says to me, "Michael, you know the drill. Give me a month or two to get organized, and then I'll bring you over to work for me."

But this time it didn't work out. I got caught stealing a miserable three-pound brick of cream cheese. Cream cheese! I don't even like the shit! I felt like I had gone crazy or something. The food service director at the hospital had no choice but to fire me. Since the new hospital where the chef was now was run by the same outfit, he couldn't hire me there. Why did I steal it? Oh, for the same reason I couldn't have moved on to a new job anyway, or anyplace else for that matter. I got that happy news the next week at the clinic.

An Empty Stool at the Gay 90's

Michael's dementia at the time of the cream cheese incident was the first manifestation of his full-blown AIDS. He grew very weak very quickly, but bouts of aggressive chemotherapy would perk him up for short periods. He was particularly eager to get some strength back for Halloween that year, and he determined that he would throw a party—one last party—for this most important of gay holidays. Since his hair had fallen out because of his treatments, he had decided to host the party in drag, although he probably would have anyway even if his health had been solid. He borrowed a cocktail dress that fit him perfectly because of his weight loss and put a frowzy blond wig on his bald head. He invited hundreds of people.

Only a couple dozen of us showed up. Hardly any of Michael's gay friends were there. They had been to too many living wakes by 1991, as the virus ravaged their community. He had no family who were on speaking terms with him. The only people who came to Michael's party were his friends from restaurants. Chefs, cooks, servers, and dishwashers gathered at Michael's place. Some were too saddened to remain there long and left early. Others got really drunk and stayed late. Michael drank soft drinks all night but was still the life of the party. Everyone worked really hard at trying to have fun, fun for Michael. When it was getting late, I found myself sitting alone with Michael as he quietly smoked a cigarette. Naturally, I tried to make cheerfully lame conversation, and I think that he appreciated the effort, but he was getting very tired and needed some more medicine. As he went to get his pills, he turned to me and said, "You know, I've probably had AIDS for years and never knew it. And I'll never know how many others I've killed."

We spoke on the phone a couple times a week after that, and in December he asked me to bring him some Christmas cookies because his appetite had been poor, and he thought some sweets would do him good. The next day, December 11, I was putting a cookie tray together when I got a call from the hospice. Michael had died overnight. He just fell asleep and never woke up. He was forty-four.

Digestif

"Okay, let's start planning the kitchen layout for this project," I announce to my sleepy Management by Menu class. Though they're all culinary students, this kind of assignment leaves them cold. They'd rather be cooking or baking or just about anything but sitting in my classroom on a frigid Minnesota morning. I can't say I blame them for that, but these days I make my living teaching, and though they don't realize it now, many of these kids will someday use this information. Thankfully, most of them at least pay polite attention.

"First of all, you need to start with your menu. What are you going to serve and how are you going to serve it?" These students have been watching food porn on TV all their lives. They're smart and creative, even passionate, but most are pretty unaware of the realities of working in a professional kitchen. I see foie gras mousses and handmade squid ink pastas in their eyes. That may come, but along the way they're sure to be spending a lot more time in the cooler scrounging for leftovers to be turned into employee meals. *That* will test their creativity.

"Obviously, if you're going to serve broiled steaks, you're going to need a broiler." And a broiler cook. Somebody who can stand over a 1,500-degree grate all night shuffling charred meat around, keeping orders and doneness straight, staying composed through the stress, and even speaking a little English. It won't be too surprising if this cook is a bit of a flake, an eccentric, even giddy at times. It goes with the territory. I hope this broiler cook won't be like the one I remember from Schiek's, who got third-degree burns on his hand when he casually leaned against the grate after ingesting two marijuana-laced brownies before his shift. Good shit.

But that broiler cook, regardless of legal status or state of mind, was also creative and passionate, albeit in different directions. Restaurant cooking was something he did in order to earn the money he needed for paints, brushes, and canvases for his real creative outlet. His paintings still show up in galleries around town. He regarded his ability to throw down, to superbly handle his station, as a sort of passport. Cooking in a restaurant allowed him to remain outside the mainstream and nurture his status as a free agent. For generations of restaurant workers, their employment allowed them to maintain a romantic, even heroic, independence. They sold their services but never their souls.

Until the price was right, that is. That price varied with the individual: weekends off, health insurance, relief for sore knees. Any or all could prompt them to change harnesses. Life intervenes. Compromises have to be made. Generally attitude, in its winsome fierceness, is all that remains.

Do I see attitude in my culinary students? Undoubtedly, but it is attitude mainly fueled by desire and professionalism. They have *chosen* life in the milieu. They know that in a nation where the vast majority cannot, or cares not to, feed

itself, their calling is valued, even venerated, and, incidentally, immune to being outsourced to India.

Some show extraordinary courage. Jessica, one of my
students from a couple of years ago, headed for Northern
California after graduation. She wanted to be as far away from
rural Wisconsin as an old Toyota would take her. She pounded
on doors, worked for free in Napa Valley restaurants, and was
eventually hired by a Michelin one-star establishment with
a movie mogul clientele. In 2005, Jessica was the *first* woman
ever hired as a line cook at this mountainside spa, and she
had to prove her worth daily in order to keep her job and her
sanity. She was hazed mercilessly but survived. The people
she works with come from all over this country and Mexico
and view their time in this elite establishment as a valuable
résumé builder. Their careers are planned, and they fully
intend to be the next generation of culinary lions. There is
no reason to believe that some of them won't do exactly that.
After all, they are working for a renowned chef who has already achieved such an exalted status.

Needless to say, this kind of single-minded dedication
is outside my experience. The restaurant world that I grew
up in was far less professional and much more haphazard.
In my own mind (admittedly softened by the passing decades), I imagine that things today are also a lot less fun. I
forget the daily effort and emotion it took to harness the
diverse energies of a revolving-door cast of renegades and
reprobates and somehow feed an indifferent public. The
product may not have always been the best, but the *process*
was fascinating.

But when I visited Jessica last summer and dined at her restaurant, it was all about the product. On a terrace overlooking a Napa Valley sunset, we were fed course after superb course until we begged the servers to stop. Each succeeding plate carried its own universe of taste, texture, and presentation. Jessica had told her boss that "her chef—the only one who's ever seen me cry" was coming to dinner, and the kitchen pulled out all the stops. By the time it was over, my wife, son, and I had sampled fourteen incredible courses and hadn't even spied dessert. It was the best meal I've ever had or am likely to have. I actually teared up at the end because it seemed, with that meal, the last word had been written in a long saga.

ACKNOWLEDGMENTS

The book you're holding came into being by a fairly circuitous route. My employer, the International Culinary School at Art Institutes International Minnesota determined that my admittedly spotty résumé could use some better credentials in the EDUCATION area and kindly sent me off to graduate school. My profound thanks for that. Having been out of college since the Pleistocene, however, I found that there was no exact fit for me in any traditional course of study. I tried out the Master of Education program, but it was filled with dispirited K-12 public school teachers comparing strategies for controlling fifth graders. Not my style.

The University of Minnesota beckoned me back with the Master of Liberal Studies (MLS) program. This course of study is for nontraditional students who construct their own interdisciplinary curriculums. The program requires the writing of a thesis, and mine was intended to be some tome about the transformational power of restaurants through the ages. As I researched this thinly documented subject, I kept coming across people and events that mirrored my own experiences. Once I started poking around in my own recollection repository, I felt the need to include some of my favorite colleagues as well. Luckily for me, my liberal studies professors approved the idea.

My thanks go out to Sarah Dennison, my advisor and taskmaster, who kept me on track during the composition of the thesis. Jeffrey M. Pilcher, a University of Minnesota professor of history by trade and a food historian of the first rank, happily pointed me in the right direction on the origins of restaurants. I'm also overwhelmingly indebted to Jack Johnson, the director of the MLS program, who reviewed the manuscript and urged me to publish the thing. Not only did he urge me, but he actually arranged for my publisher to review the finished product. Thanks, Jack, and thanks also to Jo Ellen Lundblad and Connie Hessburg of the MLS for helping me navigate through academic *terra incognita.*

Greg Britton, then director of the Minnesota Historical Society Press, was willing to take a flier on this book and get it into print. Greg left town shortly after offering me a publication contract, which I'm sure is purely coincidental, but he left me in the supremely capable hands of Mike Hanson, my boy wonder editor. Mike is not only a great editor but also a *phở* connoisseur, and I've learned much from him in both areas.

Though I had to delete all the citations from the body of this text when it went from academic thesis to whatever it is now, it would be unfair not to thank the authors of some of my sources for their diligence and hard work. Readers should seek out books by Jean-Paul Aron, Leslie Brenner, Duff Cooper, Auguste Escoffier, Priscilla Pankhurst Ferguson, Katherine Strand-Koutsky and Linda Koutsky, Patric Kuh, Harvey Levenstein, Stephen Mennell, Jeffrey M. Pilcher, Timothy Shaw, Rebecca Spang, Laura Shapiro, Reay Tannahill, and Barbara Ketchum Wheaton for the real story.

Finally, I must make mention of my family. You've met my wife, Ann, and my son, Sandy, in these pages, but my parents, Wally and Margaret, were instrumental in me just being here. They're still here too, in robust health and attitude. They gave my siblings and me a great upbringing. Never once did they criticize my career choices, though my mother was less than enthusiastic about the complete eight-place setting of pilfered Ambassador Motor Hotel china that I gave her for Christmas in 1968.

Fried *was designed & set in type by Percolator, Minneapolis. The typefaces are Filosofia, Trade Gothic, and Dorchester Script. Printed at Maple Press, York, Pennsylvania.*